WORST SEAT
IN THE HOUSE

Henry Rathbone's Front Row View
of the Lincoln Assassination

To Wilber C. Leffler,

Best wishes

CALEB JENNER STEPHENS

Caleb Stephens

WM

Published by Willow Manor Publishing
Fredericksburg, VA 22406
www.willowmanorpublishing.com

Front cover image courtesy of Jennifer Jarrett Teagle
Dust jacket and interior design courtesy of MS Illustration and Design
Images and illustrations found within are credited in the references section
Edited by Karl Monger

First published 2014

Manufactured in the United States
LCCN 2014902854
Library of Congress Catalogue-in-Publication Data
Stephens, Caleb.

Worst Seat in the House:
Henry Rathbone's Front Row View of the Lincoln Assassination

Caleb Jenner Stephens
p.cm.
Includes bibliographical references.
ISBN 978-1-939688-50-7

1.History. 2. Lincoln, Abraham. 3. Rathbone, Henry.
4. Post Traumatic Stress Disorder—PTSD. 5. Civil War

Anecdotes. I. Title

To my grandfather for passing on the love of searching through the past.

My parents for unyielding support and wisdom.

My AMAZING wife for teaching me what "unconditional" really means.

And to my children for being the driving force of every great thing I do.

CONTENTS

"There it lay upon the white china, a little black mass no bigger than the end of my finger—dull, motionless and harmless, yet the cause of such mighty changes in the world's history as we may perhaps never realize."

—Dr. Edward Curtis,
about finding the bullet that killed Lincoln,
during the autopsy.

INTRODUCTION
SETTING THE STAGE

When Abraham Lincoln was shot in April 1865, who was the man sitting behind him in the Ford's Theatre box? Not many people know. Some might know the man's name, others might recall that he was a soldier, but very few people know the full story of Henry R. Rathbone. That fateful night there were five people immediately affected by the assassination of the President, yet Major Rathbone and his wife are many times left out of the account.

Historical tapestry is composed largely of celebrated and appalling events that are cataloged, documented, and preserved, allowing future generations to look back on notable moments and to decipher the clues leading up to them. History provides people with the means to follow chain reactions of seemingly unrelated happenings and map them to a milestone in time. Experts and amateurs alike can trace inconsequential moments to major events in the historical timeline, many times finding that small details can create a domino effect, resulting in tragedy. Although these details typically are imperceptible in the moment, in hindsight they can be glaringly obvious.

This illuminates the value of studying history. Relating what is learned from the past to the present. The signs, the mistakes, the lessons, and the outcomes. In applying those lessons to our current world, the past becomes a tool. Not just notes in a book or a boring story delivered by an old curmudgeon. The commonalities between the past and present can be stunning and all historical events give us opportunity to learn. Even bad relationship choices and traffic tickets provide a precedent that our minds recall and use to adjust our future actions. The grand scale of world history should be no different than these seemingly small personal considerations. By reflecting thoughtfully and systematically on what has already happened, and relating it to contemporary problems and questions, we can build upon the work of those who have already succeeded or failed. As philosopher George Santayana famously stated,"Those who cannot remember the past are condemned to repeat it." [1]

Don't repeat mistakes made centuries earlier. Build off the success of others. Advances in most industries are made by going one step farther than the generation that came before them. But be wary. A major hurdle to relating the past to the present involves sifting through the data to distinguish the facts, the myths, the stories, and the legends. What is fact and what is fiction?

Some pieces of information begin as fact. However, after a century's worth of "The Telephone Game" they can escape the parameters of truth to become embellished fact. Over time, these minor fallacies become the truth, weaving themselves into the fabric of the stories that make up history. The stories suffer from a deformation in scope, in both an expanding and a decreasing direction. Was someone trying to appear more important, embellishing their role in an event, even just a tad? Hyperbole of character, deeds, and actions have always been a plague to those interested in historical accuracy. History, for better or for worse, rests largely in the hands of the person telling it.

One of the preeminent life-altering and course-changing events of both American and world history was the assassination of Abraham Lincoln. Since 1865, the details of the assassination have been sifted through with a fine-toothed-comb. For one hundred fifty years, everything about that tragic day and the events leading

This 34-foot tower is made of 6,800 bent aluminum book replicas. The books are all replicas of Abraham Lincoln books and can be seen at the Ford's Theatre Center for Education and Leadership.

A close up view of the Lincoln book tower. The tower is a symbol of the 15,000 and growing book titles ever written about the 16th President.

up to it have been researched and discussed. Or so you might think.

There have been more than 15,000 books written about Lincoln, the assassination, Ford's Theatre, and the aftermath of his death or Mary Todd Lincoln's decline. There are so many books about Lincoln that across the street from the site of the assassination in the Ford's Theatre Center for Education and Leadership, a tower, thirty-four feet high and eight feet around, was erected from actual size replicas of books about Abraham Lincoln.[2] Every stone in the Lincoln assassination has been overturned, some of them dozens of times. The facts of that night have been verified, then re-verified, shedding new light on Lincoln and his past every decade or so, in effect changing the historical record.

A great example of such change is the story of Clara Harris' picture that was displayed inside of Ford's Theatre. Ms. Harris was the fiancé of Major Henry R. Rathbone, and was present in the state box on assassination night. On display at Ford's

Theatre for nearly thirty years, the picture of a woman hung on the wall, the name below it: Clara Harris.

In 2002, a researcher from Maryland notified officials that the woman in the picture was, in fact, not Clara Harris. It was another woman, the identity of whom remains unknown. Yet there it was, surrounded by historians and experts every day for thirty years. The picture came from the National Archives, and was referenced and reused countless times. The National Archives is widely regarded as the pinnacle of historical record keeping, but there can never be a guarantee that the items were properly cataloged at the time they were obtained. And by no fault of the Archives, history was changed. The picture on display in Ford's Theatre has since been replaced with a correct image of Clara Harris. [3]

Incidents like the Clara Harris photograph error encourage historians and researchers to keep analyzing and to keep digging. Everything we think we know about the past can always use some fine-tuning. This anecdote proves that even information coming from the most respected sources or relying on the most diligent vetting process can still lead to falsehoods. The most important aspect of researching history is making sure the truth prevails. It's unfortunate that historical events can become undermined by hearsay or the misguided pursuits of storytellers, but it's a part of the game.

The Lincoln assassination is full of inherited errors and bad information passed down from generation to generation. The amount of abuse of the facts is cringe inducing, especially in the viral information world of today. The defective material can now be downloaded, tweeted, posted, and given a digital imprint in a matter of seconds. There is little analysis done on the news version imposed on us. Headlines pulse through our cyber feeds, filled with bias and editorializing, and consumers gorge on the bits of information, digesting them as facts. The reports are so quickly ingested that there's little time to challenge what is real and what is fiction. The information is quickly sifted through, the seemingly relevant data is logged in our brains, and the leftovers are swept aside as we move on to the next item on the day's agenda.

As a society, we normally don't have the time it would take to clarify the information we take as fact. Verifying the accuracy of information is time consuming, and because of this we've grown more dependent on the "experts". In an ironic turn of events, as we've put more faith in news sources, the news sources have simultaneously become less reliable. Yellow journalism is alive and well. Amateur and professional news sources alike devote more time to sensationalism than they do to research or verification of facts. The onus, however, remains on the individual. We need to become more diligent regarding the information we read, hear, or even see. We now live in a world that we can barely believe with our own eyes. People are required to stay consciously aware of the source of information and put in a little more detective work before assimilating it. Being aware and more vigilant is the first step.

The detective work is the hard part, but it can be the most rewarding. Searching for nuggets of information can become an obsession - hunting for a missing piece of data, a letter, a note, a signature - anything to link two unrelated items together and provide the missing piece of the puzzle. Sometimes the information is simply not there. Not every person in history led the sort of life whose every action was deemed important enough to document. Or the documentary records could have been lost. Possibly destroyed. Some people fluctuate between the two worlds, popping up throughout history a few times, only to vanish soon after. Henry and Clara Rathbone lived this type of life.

Married two years after the assassination on April 14, 1865, the couple simply found themselves at the wrong the place at the wrong time on April 14th, 1865. After the Lincolns' invitation to Ford's Theatre was declined by many others, it was Clara and Henry who finally accepted. Unbeknownst to them, accompanying the invitation was a pass to a life riddled with anguish, mental illness, regret, and sadness. A pivotal night and turning point in American history became the catalyst for a life filled with tribulation. A decision that seemed simple in the moment, an insignificant choice, ended up having immense historical repercussions.

For all the retrospective consideration the assassination has been afforded, the amount of attention given to the Rathbones is oddly minimal. It isn't that the amount of attention given to Lincoln is unwarranted. I don't believe there has ever been another American President who met his nation's expectations of leadership, fairness, and fortitude more than Abraham Lincoln. However, for two people who witnessed and were within arm's reach of this great man's death, it's odd how their lives have been historically glossed over. The couple is almost ghost-like in many historical accounts, seen for a moment and recognized only when reminded.

In comparison to the twenty-four-hour news cycle we live in today, this exception is both refreshing and puzzling. Henry and Clara would be instant celebrities in the 21st century. Imagine the degree of news coverage their story would win today. They were a young engaged couple, also step-siblings, with front row seats to the assassination of the President of the United States. Not just any President either, but one who presided over the Army that had effectively ended the Civil War. While Lincoln's approval was mixed and beleaguered throughout his presidency, Robert E. Lee's surrender on April 9 provided a welcomed relief of Lincoln's judgment. Six days later Lincoln died and was instantly immortalized. His life became legend and his status elevated to national hero.

Yet in 1865, there were scarcely any interviews with Henry and Clara. There were no live reports outside of Rathbone's home, reporting on his recovery. Clara wasn't interviewed in gossip columns. She didn't discuss her relationship with Mary Todd Lincoln, or how she consoled her dear friend through that somber night. Today their names would be perpetually before our eyes. A red banner, scrolling nonstop across the screen, would give hourly updates on the Rathbone couple. I'm not condoning celebrity as a result of tragic events. It's simply interesting to note the differences in the press, media and society.

Then, as easily as the couple was nonchalantly plucked from relative obscurity on assassination night, Henry and Clara were just as easily cast aside after the tragedy. They were duly mentioned in passing in nearly every account of the evening. Typically, though, their mention merited little more than footnotes, as authors strived to stay within the confines of historical reference requirements. In many accounts you can virtually sense the editor's reluctance at wasting copy space on the couple. And in nearly all discussions and newspapers, as soon as the dying Lincoln was settled in the short bed in the Peterson house, any mention of Henry and Clara is scarce to be found. Leaving the President in a strange bed, the couple traveled down the chaotic dirt road of 10th Street, moving onto a lingering tragedy to be shared by them alone.

The historical amnesia surrounding Henry Rathbone and Clara Harris is disappointing. Not only is their story engaging, anecdotal, intriguing, and full of notable historical figures, but following their lives gives us a glimpse into modern concerns. As senseless acts of violence and unspeakable crimes committed by the mentally ill seem to increase at an alarming rate, we can look back one hundred fifty years for clues. We can follow the progression of a man that

ASSASSINATION OF PRESIDENT A.LINCOLN.

One of the many illustrations of President Lincoln's assassination. This image shows John Wilkes Booth with both the gun and knife drawn.
Source: Library of Congress

dealt with a form of post-traumatic stress disorder rarely seen.

From the Civil War and the firsthand experience of having Abraham Lincoln murdered five feet from him, Henry Rathbone lived the remaining forty-six years of his life replaying the events of that night in his mind. Questions and regret undoubtedly plagued his thoughts.

What could I have done differently?

Should I have seen John Wilkes Booth earlier?

Could I have restrained Booth despite my knife wound?

Could I have saved the President of the United States?

As a man of the gallant nineteenth century and a decorated soldier who had witnessed the deaths of hundreds, Rathbone dealt with this ultimate failure alone. It was a struggle mentally, physically, and emotionally. He was the only man in the world that night with the opportunity to protect, save, and instantly avenge the life of Abraham Lincoln - an extraordinarily heavy cross to bear for any man. What lessons can be learned from the life of Rathbone, leading up to and after the assassination? What can be learned of how he was treated by his family, friends, and society?

He was allowed to live while a greater man died.

What was Rathbone's penance?

Did a day ever pass that Rathbone didn't hear that gunshot ring in his ears? In what ways was Rathbone hardened after the assassination? Or was he simply a spoiled rich kid, born with a silver spoon and unable to cope with true adversity?

Later in life, as he frittered away his final twenty-eight years in an insane asylum, Rathbone refused to speak of Lincoln. He refused to speak of Clara or her murder. The two defining moments of his life were lost to him. Exiled from his broken mind or locked away in a location so remote even Rathbone chose not to navigate there. Always on edge, never at rest, the man with the worst seat in the house on April 14, 1865, wasn't going to be ambushed again. Looking back at the life of Henry Rathbone, it's hard to not put yourself in his position that fateful night. What would you have done?

How would you have dealt with failing the entire world?

1
CLAPPED IN THE MADHOUSE

Even in death, Henry and Clara Rathbone were afforded little peace. Somewhere lost in the city cemetery, Stadtfriedhof Engesohde, of Hanover, Germany, the couple's bodies lay ignored in lightly marked graves. From 1883 to 1911, Clara rested alone in the double grave, awaiting her husband and murderer. However, just as she had in life, Clara suffered in silence. Alone in the German earth she was far away from her family in a foreign world, thousands of miles from her beloved Albany, N.Y. and her adopted home of Washington, D.C. She could only sit by and wait for Henry as he lived on.

Henry was also alone. Committed to a nearby insane asylum, he struggled through an existence filled with shadows and uncertainty until after twenty-eight years of loneliness and being apart, Henry finally joined Clara in 1911. The lovers were again side-by-side. At last they had found a pittance of rest together, lodging in the dirt through the mild seasons of Hanover.

Henry's mind was finally at ease, and the haunting images of the Lincoln assassination and Clara's murder could torment him no more. For Clara, she could be near to the man she loved without worry of upsetting the fragile ego Henry clung to in life.

The lost souls once again traveled together through death, just as they did through life. First as brother and sister, then as husband and wife, and finally ending as murderer and victim, theirs was an unconventional relationship. But it was theirs.

During their time in the German cemetery, there was little record of Henry or Clara's children, family, or friends visiting either of the graves. So, in the North German earth they lay. Undisturbed. Unvisited. Forgotten.

Back in the United States, for the few who still remembered Henry and Clara, the couple undoubtedly brought back painful memories. The Rathbone couple was no longer remembered merely for being witnesses to Lincoln's assassination. They now had top billing in a tragedy all their own. After Clara's death and Henry's arrest, the couple's children moved to Cleveland, Ohio, where they were raised by their uncle, William Hamilton Harris. All three children grew to lead successful and happy lives, the oldest son, Henry Riggs Rathbone, later became a U.S. Congressman for the state of Illinois. Whether the children's success was due to the seclusion and avoidance of their parents' past or in spite of it, the children were able to move beyond the haunting family history and flourish as adults.

The horrific scene the children dealt with was relived as Henry's death was splashed across the front pages of the American newspapers in 1911. The death of the madman and wife-killer brought with it a disinterment of the details of Clara's murder twenty-eight years earlier. Henry's attendance at the Lincoln assassination was noted as the probable impetus of his derangement, and this became the last footnote on the man that wrestled with John Wilkes Booth. To most he was a lunatic, a murderer, and a failed hero. And it was this man who was laid next to Clara in the Hanover cemetery, there to enjoy each other's company for four decades.

Their rest was short lived, because in 1952, just over forty years after Henry's death, the couple was wrenched from their slumber. Every year, following normal procedure, the Engesohde cemetery completes a review of their records in an attempt to determine whether or not any graves can be reused.

Engesohde Cemetery in Hanover, Germany. The burial site for Henry and Clara Rathbone.

According to the cemetery, Henry and Clara's graves had a dearth of visitation or family correspondence over the years and the cemetery records showed the Rathbone sites seemed to be forgotten by anyone who may have known the couple. Up until 2013, the story that circulated about the remains of Henry and Clara was that the bodies were exhumed, fully decomposed, and the remains destroyed, their existence wiped off the face of the Earth. But thanks to the efforts of a researcher living in Germany, it was discovered the cemetery's procedure is not to destroy or dispose of remains. The bodies are simply relocated lower in the ground.[1]

The way in which people may lose their burial sites stems from the fact that burial sites at Engesohde cemetery are purchased for a fixed amount of time. After this time is up, another fee must be paid in order to extend the amount of time. For example, the fee in 2012 for a burial plot was $1,596 US for a fixed period of 20 years.[2] In the Rathbones' case, after Henry died in August 1911, assuming they started the countdown the next year and the couple was afforded two fixed periods, their forty years would have ended in 1952.

It was that same year their bodies were moved. No one paid to renew or extend their gravesite after that time, and because burial sites were needed the Rathbones were forgotten. However, although they were forgotten, we now know they were not lost. According to the cemetery, they are still in the same location, just lower in the ground. When a grave is to be reused, the original occupants are exhumed, the grave is deepened, the original occupants are replaced, and the new casket is placed on top. When this process takes place the original gravestone or marker is removed and a new one with the new occupants name is put in its place.

Such treatment was nothing new for the Rathbones. The couple had a knack for disappearing or being overshadowed. Although never of their own accord, they always found a way to fall through the cracks of history's floorboards. The events that transpired after Abraham Lincoln's assassination followed such a pattern. Besides Mary Todd Lincoln, Clara and Henry were the only two people to witness the killing of the President, yet they were barely heard from after that night. Henry and Clara's sworn affidavits during the assassination conspiracy trial are the only true firsthand accounts from the couple. Very little press regarding the couple's whereabouts or their wellbeing exists. Until Clara's murder eighteen years later, the couple lived in relative obscurity. In any story regarding the Lincoln assassination, Henry and Clara were mentioned only in passing. They were dealt with as an afterthought. In fictional paraphrase, most papers and articles summed up the Rathbones' involvement as, "Oh, by the way, Major Rathbone and Miss Harris were also there... but only because General Grant and his wife couldn't make it."

Even today, the official pamphlet handed out to tourists at Ford's Theater, reveals little mention of the couple. The detailed pictorial timeline in the pamphlet handed out to every visitor describes the events of that night, yet the image shows no sign of the Rathbones sitting inside the Presidential box. The picture shows only Abraham and Mary Todd.[3] Simply put, their involvement is considered optional. They have become ghosts of history.

In the basement of Ford's Theatre, a museum enlightens visitors in wondrous detail. All things Lincoln are covered, including his presidency, the assassination, and the hunt for John Wilkes Booth. Henry Rathbone and Clara Harris are mentioned five times amongst the hundreds of relics, artifacts, and detailed descriptions. And where they are mentioned they are never discussed in any detail. Even the multitudes of assailants involved in the conspiracy who had no contact whatsoever with Lincoln himself are afforded more attention. While understandable that visitors aren't flocking thousands of miles to visit the spot where Major Rathbone received a knife wound in the arm, it's important to question how so little is discussed of the only man to attempt to stand up to history's most famous assassin.

Approximately twenty miles southeast of the Rathbones' gravesite is the town of Hildesheim. One of the oldest cities in Northern Germany, Hildesheim is a picturesque town with a beautiful mix of Gothic, Baroque, Rococo, and Romanesque architecture styles. The city is a popular tourist attraction for visitors desiring a simple and serene experience. The historic marketplace is a consummate example of the blend of old world charm and serene magnetism that Hildesheim breathes.[4]

On the northwest end of town sits the angelic St. Michael's cathedral. A breathtaking example of early Romanesque architecture, the church has a long and tortured history of its own. Dating back to its construction in 1031, the church was built under the watchful eye of Bishop Bernward, the Bishop of Hildesheim. In addition, to his church duties, Bernward was a man of many interests, but he had a deep appreciation for and education in architecture and art. He used these talents to design buildings that still influence architectural design today, St. Michael's Cathedral being one such example. Every year students and tourists flock to Hildesheim to inspect and consume the uniqueness of Bernward's designs.[5]

It's among these inspiring designs and architectural phenomenon that Rathbone lived his last years. In the vast and manicured gardens of St. Michael's Cathedral is where Henry R. Rathbone took his strolls and let a haunted mind breathe. Ambivalently walking the grounds of the Ottonian church, Henry was given a long and loose leash at the asylum. The immense building adjacent to St. Michael's was the Michaelis monastery. For hundreds of years before Henry's arrival the monastery was a place of prayer and residence for the monks and priests of St. Michael's. In 1827, the monastery and cloisters were transformed into a makeshift insane asylum and madhouse.[6] And it was this asylum that opened its doors to Henry after tragedy struck the Rathbone family—again—in the early morning hours of Christmas Eve 1883. Not long after the tragedy Henry began his residency in the hauntingly beautiful monastery next to St. Michael's, where he remained until his death in 1911.

The events that brought Henry to the asylum transpired during the Rathbone family's residence in Hanover, the place

St. Michael's Cathedral in Hildesheim, Germany. Henry lived the final twenty-seven years of life in the asylum next to this church.

they had chosen to further their children's education. It's commonly noted that Henry was the U.S. Consul to Hanover. However, records show this not to be true. Not only was Henry not the Consul to Hanover, he was never the U.S. Consul to any city. Despite multiple attempts to obtain such an occupation, he was always refuted. This incorrect fact seems to stem from a mix-up between Henry and his brother Jared Lawrence Rathbone, who was the U.S. Consul to Paris in 1887 during the Cleveland Administration.[7]

The family was known to travel from Europe to America multiple times throughout the year, but Hanover was to be the last stop for Henry and Clara. Following the horrific actions taken by a mentally ill man on Christmas Eve morning, the couple's final chapter was written.

Henry awoke early that morning in a fit of worry, brutally murdered Clara, and then attempted suicide by stabbing himself five times. He was promptly found insane by the German courts, and immediately thereafter the monastery turned asylum became his home for the remaining twenty-eight years of his life. The symbolism of Clara's death was not overlooked. By shooting Clara and stabbing her, then turning the knife on himself, Henry's actions overtly mimicked the deed of John Wilkes Booth eighteen years prior. Shot and stabbed to death, Clara lay lifeless on her bed when the German police arrived. Henry bled profusely on the floor nearby, screaming of men hiding behind the paintings that adorned the bedroom walls.

It was after being declared insane and unable to stand trial that Henry was moved to the Hildesheim Asylum for the Criminally Insane.[8] From all accounts, he lived something close to a luxurious lifestyle. It's noted from reports and records that Major Rathbone was given near free roam of the church and monastery grounds and had a daily schedule unlike any standard patient. His time there quite possibly entailed the most peaceful moments of his adult life, despite the fact that he lived in constant fear of the men that wanted to persecute and torture him.[9]

In his life, Henry had led men through Civil War battles and survived firsthand a conspired assassination attempt, so it's not surprising that his mental illness potpourri included a heaping dose of paranoia. Henry persisted, up to the last days of his life, that there were men out to get him. It was an argument that began soon after the murder of his wife. He was convinced it was the work of conspirators, no doubt, at least in his mind, a duplication of the detailed and organized actions of the same men that killed Lincoln and attacked Senator William H. Seward in 1865. Allowing such experiences to fester in one's mind without getting qualified treatment or discussing it keeps the trauma alive, and as long as trauma survives it remains a threat. Continuous rumination on past events and mistakes is a major symptom of post-traumatic stress disorder (PTSD).

Individuals dealing with PTSD find it difficult to turn their focus on finding a solution as they are constantly and consistently brought back to the past traumatic event. Those who suffer from PTSD ask themselves the same questions over and over, reliving the same horrible moments that they need to let go of. The specific type of rumination that relates to failure is referred to as state rumination. Persons with this affliction have feelings of regret and failure that linger constantly. These thoughts come and go throughout life, always persisting, brought to mind by even the subtlest unrelated triggers. Henry Rathbone suffered these ruminations from Lincoln's assassination, not only causing him to second-guess his actions from decades past, but also affecting his daily life choices.

It wasn't the first time someone connected with the Lincoln assassination had ended up in an insane asylum. The most well-known afflicted was Lincoln's wife, Mary Todd. She became the most famous living casualty of the assassination and in combination with the deaths of her children caused her sanity to be debated for years. Her son, Robert, ended up finally admitting Mary to an insane asylum on May 20, 1875, after repeated instances of questionable acts by Mary. Robert had her admitted for her own safety as well as to give him a chance to live a less complicated life. At the time of her admittance, Robert stated his actions were under the counsel of six physicians who advised that the longer he waited to commit her, the more he was establishing himself as "morally responsible for some very probable tragedy." [10]

Mary Todd did not stay long in the asylum, however. She vehemently denied the allegations of her insanity and with the aid of lawyers was able to parlay her efforts into a release. After only four months in the asylum she was discharged under the care of her sister. Then on June 15, 1876 she was officially declared sane by the courts.

Another case of insanity related to the assassination was the man who shot and killed John Wilkes Booth. In 1887, Boston Corbett found his way to the Topeka Asylum for the Insane. Corbett's case is slightly different from his counterparts, however, as he may have had previous mental damage from his years spent as a hatter before the Civil War. Hatters in the 1800s were constantly exposed to mercury during the process of turning fur into felt. Symptoms of mercury poisoning include anxiety and depression. Similar to Mary, Corbett's stay in the asylum was short as well. In 1888, after only a year in the asylum, Corbett succeeded in escaping. His whereabouts after the escape are uncertain and have been debated since. [11]

When looking back on these cases it's important to remember that the science of mental health in 1865 was still in its infancy. At the time of the assassination very little was known about the human brain and how it responds to trauma. Karl Ludwig Kahlbaum was the first to begin the classification of mental illnesses, but not until the late 1800s. [12] At the time that Henry suffered his illness the common practice was to "group all mental disorders as forms of either 'MANIA' or 'MELONCHOLIA'. [13] This labeling corresponds with the account given by Henry's relatives. Those who knew Henry the best reported that after Lincoln's death he suffered from deep bouts of melancholy.

In their final years, Henry and Clara had only each other for consolation. There's no record of them discussing the assassination night, but no other person on Earth could fully relate to that experience. Clara was the only person Henry could truly feel comfortable with, knowing that she alone really

Boston Corbett
The man that shot John Wilkes Booth.
Source: National Archives

understood. Henry probably felt that discussing it with anyone else was futile. Who could possibly fathom what it was like to have lived through such a tragedy?

Unfortunately, Henry grew quieter over the years. His disposition, attitude, and paranoia intensified, and while Henry battled his inner demons, Clara was emotionally isolated. For the last few years of her life, she had to do without the complete attention of her husband. She could confide in her sister and other close relatives about the difficulties of living with Henry, but there were no options for professional advice. When Henry's attitude worsened, Clara entertained the idea of leaving her husband, but in the end, she stayed by his side. Her devotion was for two reasons. The first was the fear that a separation would put a social blight on her family's name, and Clara was worried how

In this image of the assassination you can see Booth hiding in shadows and Rathbone behind Clara, only a few feet away from the killer.
Source: National Archives

friends might react. But the second and most important reason was that she was dearly devoted to her husband. Clara felt it was her obligation as a wife to care for Henry. She believed that she was living only that she might watch over him.[14]

We can assume that the couple's three children suffered similarly and were never able to fully connect with their father. While Henry's devotion to his family was witnessed by all who knew the Rathbones, Henry was never the man he intended to be. His children may have provided respite from his disease, and undoubtedly he turned to them in times of mental desperation. Maybe looking upon their childhood innocence enabled Henry to escape from his internal despair, if only temporarily. But Henry's mind couldn't pardon his inability to follow through with the unspoken duty he had shirked on April 14, 1865.

As a man and an Army officer, when John Wilkes Booth entered the Presidential box, Henry was given the rare opportunity to become a legend. He might have been known the world around, giving the Rathbone family name international recognition. Not only did Rathbone allow Booth to kill Lincoln, however, but to add insult to injury, he let the assassin break free after having him in his grasp.

The very idea of a Shakespearean actor overpowering and winning a fight against a trained soldier seemed on its face a ludicrous one. How degrading must that have been? How could Henry not have seen Booth enter the Presidential box? He was only seven feet from the door. Sitting behind the other three in the box that night, Henry rested on a sofa that was pressed against the back wall. His view of the stage was mediocre at best, barely enabling him to see that night's performance of *Our American Cousin*. It was quite possibly the worst seat in the house. He sat behind Lincoln, Mary Todd, and his fiancée, Clara, and the majority of the audience probably didn't even know he was there. Especially after General Grant had been expected and the audience had found him in his stead, Henry was paid little mind to.

What might someone who couldn't see the play and couldn't be seen by anyone have been doing? Late at night in the theater and while resting on a sofa, how could Henry have missed seeing Booth enter the box?

The customary assumption is that Rathbone was watching the play. Rathbone himself stated that he "was intently observing the proceedings upon the stage, with my back toward the door."[15] While we have no reason to question Major Rathbone's word, looking closer at the details, it's hard to imagine Rathbone was fully devoted to that night's performance.

As the story goes, Rathbone tussled with John Wilkes Booth after hearing the "discharge of a pistol." Henry "instantly sprang toward him," grabbing at Booth and receiving a life-threatening gash down his left arm.[16] Booth was able to wrestle free and jump from the box to the stage, escaping out the back. It's a sound story, cut and dried. However, there are other details and facts that may support a different version of the events. Maybe Rathbone had more of an opportunity to prevent Lincoln's death than is typically assumed. These new details will be discussed later as the focus of the assassination night is brought into view and the full account is dissected. These alternate theories may help us better understand the mental anguish and guilt that faced Henry Rathbone for the rest of his life. Having the burden of the President's death on your head would undoubtedly haunt your mind in unimaginable ways.

The idea that Henry Rathbone could have prevented the assassin from delivering the fatal shot isn't an attack on his character. It's simply one more strange coincidence in a long list of odd occurrences that became incorporated into the story of the assassination night. Everything had to go off in a specific way for Booth to reach the President. On April 14, 1865, destiny proved to be the worst enemy of all, and in the process of its unfolding the legend of Abraham Lincoln found its final chapter.

Anyone finding themselves in the same scenario may have acted the same way as Rathbone. It could have happened to anyone, but that night Henry Rathbone seemed to be on the wrong side of fate. General Grant himself, the man originally destined for Rathbone's seat, may have reacted in a similar fashion. How was Rathbone to know of John Wilkes Booth's intentions? The

John Wilkes Booth (1838 - 1865)
The man that killed Abraham Lincoln.
Source: National Archives

attack happened so quickly. Is it even possible he could have reacted in any other way?

Whatever the actual events of that night, there's no changing the outcome. We can only process all the information critically and objectively and form educated opinions as to what transpired. But it's important not to forget the man who sat by Lincoln's side that night. The struggles he endured following the assassination and how ultimately the events, or the memories thereof, became too much for him to handle. Major Rathbone and Miss Harris would be the final victims of Booth's wrath. After Henry took Clara's life, he was damned to a life in asylum. Henry's home now not only was away from his children, family, and friends, but also was far from the city settings he was accustomed to in Albany and Washington. Rathbone's mind was a shell of what it once was as he wandered the fields of a monastery thousands of miles from anyone who still cared.

Henry's struggle with post-traumatic stress, paranoia, and schizophrenia was a mighty weight to bear in the mid-19th century. Even today doctors are divided on how best to treat such disorders. Symptoms of disorders are so closely related, it makes for difficult diagnoses. Because of this, in connection with a patient's fear of full disclosure, false diagnoses are a part of the process. Prescriptions are signed for as doctors try beating mental illness into submission with pills and therapy sessions can be a long process of trust and understanding. The acceptance for treatment of mental illness has come a long way recently, both in public perception and patient willingness. However, there is still much work to be done to understand the complexity of the human mind.

In 1883, therapy and prescriptions were not an option. There were no pills to calm the storm raging inside Henry's mind. There was no one he could talk to who understood the complexities and nuances of the human brain or the related body ailments he suffered from.

To better understand Henry Rathbone and his actions, it's important to examine his entire life, including his childhood and his role in the Civil War. Then after looking deeper into the

Lincoln assassination and his later family life we can follow his slow descent into madness, and at that point a better argument can be made for what Henry was dealing with.

As with most arguments, it's important to have as much information as possible before coming to a conclusion. Was the assassination the chief reason he succumbed to insanity? Did he have a mental illness his entire life? If so, maybe the assassination was the last straw, giving his illness the nudge that threw his mind into a perpetual state of digression? How does PTSD affect someone such as Rathbone? When you are the only man in position to come between Abraham Lincoln and his assassin, what impact does that have on the rest of your life?

2
CHILDHOOD AND LIFE IN ALBANY

Henry Reed Rathbone was born into vastly different circumstances than his theater acquaintance Abraham Lincoln. It's important to evaluate where these men came from and juxtapose them against one another. Not only to compare and contrast their achievements and shortfalls, but to gain some insight into the events and environments that molded them into the men they became. For instance, whereas Abraham Lincoln was the son of a poor farmer and grew up in the harsh wilderness environments of Kentucky and Indiana, Henry was handed a life of opportunity. His upbringing did not involve a struggle to win connections and earn clout. In meeting and overcoming adversity, which became a theme in his life, Lincoln learned how to confront and overcome hardship and disappointment and grew as person. Henry, on the other hand, was never forced to face the cruelty of the world head on. He was welcomed into life, handed the proverbial silver spoon, and never contended with the imposed restrictions that came with living without money.

Henry's father, Jared Lewis Rathbone, was a successful businessman and politician by the time Henry was born in 1837. In the growing New York capital of Albany, Jared Rathbone was able to offer his son as many open doors as a young man could need. Jared was well known in Albany due to his ownership of a successful wholesale grocery and general merchandising business. Owing to his business and his congenial qualities, Jared Rathbone was well liked and well regarded in the capital. In fact, due to the efforts of Jared and the hard work and ingenuity of the entire extended Rathbone family, their name carried great respect and power in Albany.[1,2]

Jared's brothers, Joel and Valentine Rathbone, were similarly successful in business, and the Rathbone surname quickly became equated with distinguish and wealth. Valentine was the first of the Rathbone brothers to move to Albany from their birthplace in Salem, Connecticut. It was Valentine who started the grocery business on the Hudson River waterfront, where Jared would soon join him, and the brothers would work together for several years. In 1832, due to bad health, Valentine handed

The Rathbone Stove Exhibition. Started by Henry's uncle, Joel Rathbone, the Rathbone stoves were just one example of the many businesses the Rathbone family succeeded at. - J.S. Van Buren, Albany, NY (1888)
Courtesy of Albany Institute of History & Art

Watercolor painting of Jared Lewis Rathbone, Henry's father. Made from life by John Godin of Washington.
Source: Albany Chronicles

the business over to Jared. One year later, Valentine passed away. In later years, Valentine's sons, John Finley Rathbone and Lewis Rathbone, would continue the tradition and become as successful as the original three Rathbone brothers.[3]

Joel Rathbone was the last of the three brothers to come to Albany. He worked for his older brothers first at the grocery store, and then in 1827 he ventured in a different direction. With the help of Valentine and Jared, and in partnership with Thomas Heermans, Joel began producing and selling iron stoves. At the time the market for iron stoves was flourishing as homes and businesses began utilizing them to replace fireplaces. Over time,

Old Albany Capital Building. Henry's home on 28 Eagle street was directly across from the capital.
Source: The state government for 1879

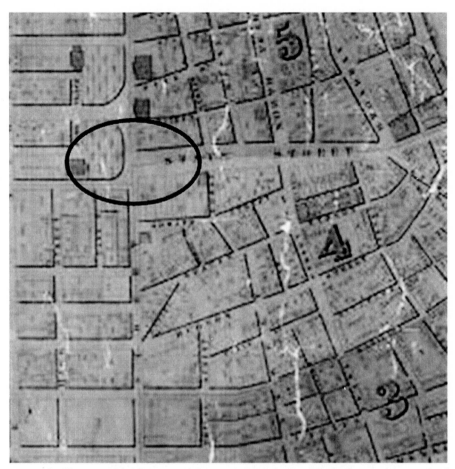

Map of Albany 1843 (Corner of State and Eagle St. Circled). At then end of State street is the Hudson River.
Source: Maps of New York City and State / Cities and towns, A-Z

Joel created one the largest names in the world in iron stoves and amassed a great fortune.[4] As his brother continued to succeed in the business world, Jared Lewis Rathbone became quite the renaissance man. After serving as city councilman for several terms, Jared was appointed mayor of Albany on January 21, 1839, after the sitting mayor died.[5]

This appointment is of historical interest as Jared Lewis became the last appointed mayor in Albany. In 1840, he became the first elected mayor in Albany, after the city adopted the requirement of a popular vote for the mayoral seat. In the city's first election, Jared L. Rathbone was shown the love and admiration of the citizens of Albany. He won the mayoral election, on the Whig party ticket, defeating Erastus Corning by a vote of 2466 to 2099.[6] Although his time as mayor of Albany came to an end in 1841, Jared Lewis continued his service to his city. Jared Lewis went on to diversify his leadership talents by becoming president of the Albany Medical College, director of the State Bank of Albany, and director of the Albany Insurance Company, helping grow the Rathbone name into even higher regard.

Along the journey of building his fortune and business, Jared Lewis met a young woman by the name of Pauline Noyes Pinney. There is no record of how long the courtship lasted, but by the time the couple married on June 26, 1834, Jared Lewis was forty-three years old whereas Pauline was still a young woman of twenty-five, making Jared Lewis eighteen years her senior.

Three years after their marriage, on July 1, 1837, Henry Reed Rathbone was born. The first-born son, Henry was the heir apparent to Jared Lewis' legacy. When his father first became mayor of Albany in 1839, Henry was only eighteen months old, and throughout Henry's entire life he never knew his father as anything but successful and a man of high reputation.

Life in Albany for young Henry must have been grand. Looking back, the accomplishments and improvements in industry and society during Henry's time were revolutionary. To Henry and the residents of Albany, however, it was just everyday life. The Rathbone home at 28 Eagle Street sat right in the center of all the action. Living in the nerve center of Albany provided many opportunities for Henry to witness the nonstop improvements of the 19th century. Situated on the corner of State and Eagle Streets, Henry's home was directly across the street from the Capitol building, providing him constant entertainment as politicians and businessmen cavorted in the streets. With Jared Lewis having his hands in many of the city's activities, their home's central location undoubtedly provided the opportunity for many visitors and social gatherings. To the south-east, only a half-mile away, the Hudson River bustled with traders, and by

1865 the largest lumber industry in the nation was in action only a couple of blocks away from Henry's front door.[7]

By the time Henry was born, Albany was the ninth largest urban area in the United States.[8] The city of was full of great minds, politicians, and businessmen. The range of industries proliferating in Albany was as diverse as any place in the world. In the world of science and technology, Joseph Henry built the first ever electric motor in 1829 at Albany Academy, a prestigious school on Eagle Street, a five-minute walk from the Rathbone home.[9] The completion of the Erie Canal in 1825 was a major growth impetus for the city, as the Albany Basin on the north side of town formed the end of the canal. This meant that all ship traffic coming from the Great Lakes and heading to New York City had to pass through Albany. The new canal brought an immense number of new residents to Albany, as did the advent of the New York Central Railroad. At age sixteen, Henry was witness to Albany becoming one of America's leaders in the railroad industry when the city became the hub of the New York Central Railroad in 1853. The railroad utilized the broad-ranging talents of the Albany workforce in housing its headquarters, repair shops, and cattle yards, bringing with them the nation's wealthiest men.[10]

This is the world that oversaw Henry Rathbone's development. He was molded by the bustle of city life and the ever-evolving technology and prosperity. As the only son of one of Albany's greatest citizens his childhood included little adversity. Comparing this lifestyle to Lincoln's country upbringing, the forces of perception and relativity come into play. To Abraham Lincoln, daily toil and struggle was a necessity of life. He was required by his father to assist with the chores and jobs that were needed to keep the family fed. He was depended on as a vital part of the family, a cog at work in a functioning system. Rathbone, however, was most likely just a voyeur to his father's world. The food on the table came from the Grace of God, requiring no work from Henry's hands. Education was a priority for the Rathbone family, whereas Lincoln's father felt that it got in the way of Abraham's chores.

The argument of nature versus nurture finds its way easily into the lives of Abraham Lincoln and Henry Rathbone. Was Henry's lifestyle an invitation to future despair and mental illness? Would Henry Rathbone have handled the great stressors of his life more successfully if his youth had been more challenging? Although these questions are best considered talking points, as the actuality of them cannot be ascertained, they give us a deeper understanding of the foundation of Rathbone's psyche. Through investigation of Rathbone's world from start to finish, we see how Henry fit into his surroundings.

As a child, Henry was the apple of his father's eye. Jared and Pauline had a son prior to Henry's birth, Charles Rathbone, but the boy died before reaching the age of two. After dealing with this heartbreak the Rathbone parents surely understood the fragility of life and appreciated Henry all the more. They undoubtedly made a conscious effort not to take their child's life for granted. As with most only children, it's imagined that he was doted on with great interest and provided all the trappings a child could want.

Henry's arrangement changed on September 28, 1844, one month after his seventh birthday, with the birth of his brother Jared Lawrence Rathbone. Although there is no record of how young Henry reacted to the arrival of his brother, he now had to share the attention of his parents, an unwelcome undertaking by many siblings. It's known that later in life, Henry dealt with issues of jealousy, and it was something that became a constant burden on his relationship with Clara. And not only did he have to split the attention of his parents, but this new brother was to share the same first name as his father. Being pushed out of the "Jared Rathbone" club may have given Henry his first nudge into the realm of rejection.

3
FATHERS AND CLARA

The first major loss in Henry Rathbone's life was his father. On May 13, 1845, Jared Lewis Rathbone passed away at the age of fifty-four.[1] At the time of Jared Lewis' death Henry was eight years old and no doubt was deeply affected by the loss. As a man of success and distinction, Jared Lewis cast a shadow as large as any man in the eyes of Henry. Jared was a role model of success to Albany, but a guiding light and role model of life to Henry. Upon his father's death Henry lost the guidance of a man who could teach him the ins and outs of business, politics, and influencing people, but ultimately, Henry lost the greatest mentor a boy can have. His father.

Jared Lewis' death was the result of pleurisy,[2] an inflammation of the cavity surrounding the lungs. A commonly fatal disease up to the mid-20th century, pleurisy is caused by many conditions. The most common is viral infection. The symptoms of pleurisy can include stabbing pains in the chest, coughing, fever, painful breathing, and weight loss. Young Henry must have watched his father's deterioration with confused eyes, not understanding the transformation from the confidant man he once knew into someone helpless in the face of a plethora of symptoms. Even if Henry tried to escape the vision of his deteriorating father, Jared's violent coughing fits would have echoed through the house, hunting down the young boy and remind him of his father's impending death.

Records do not show for how long Henry's father struggled with pleurisy, but in May 1845, Jared Lewis took his last stabbing breath. His body was laid to rest in the Albany Rural Cemetery days later. In a symbol of the high esteem in which Jared Lewis Rathbone was held, his tomb was designed after that of Scipio Barbatus[3], the Roman general.

After Jared's death, Henry became the non-official head of household. Although there was little an eight-year-old boy could do to fill the shoes of his father in this situation, his life dramatically changed. Prior to Jared Lewis' death, Henry had scarcely any responsibilities. Henry wouldn't have been expected to take on the normal duties of a man of those times, but unspoken burdens weighed on the young boy. Henry was now the oldest male presence at 28 Eagle Street and as such he became the impromptu teacher and paternal figure for his eight-month-old brother, Jared Lawrence. The dichotomy of Henry's situation was that he was old enough to perceive the issues now facing his mother but still too young to appropriately discuss her emotions.

Tomb of Roman General Lucius Cornelius Scipio Barbatus. The tomb of Jared Rathbone was created in a matching style.

And as his mother coped with her own burdens, Henry now had nowhere else to turn in dealing with his own internal turmoil.

Henry probably felt lost and confused, wondering what was to become of his family. Fortunately, Jared Lewis didn't leave his family and son completely in the lurch. At the time of his father's death, Henry inherited two hundred thousand dollars from his family's estate.[4] This was an enormous sum of money for a child, equal to approximately 6.2 million dollars today.[5] Although the money provided Rathbone with a cushion that would last into adulthood, he was determined to make something of himself by his own means.

As a man who dealt with overwhelmingly traumatic stress as an adult, it's important to analyze the first portentous circumstance of his childhood. People are shaped by the moments that make up their lives. Moments big and small, memorable and forgettable, all carve out little crevices in our life paths. Every decision has the possibility to impact the person they become. Every choice has multiple and imperceivable branches, spreading out in different directions and creating the various roads our life can take. Sometimes these molding moments are simply circumstances of nature. There is no control over them. Jared Lewis' death was that type of moment for Henry.

It's unlikely that Henry suffered from any sort of post-traumatic stress as a result of his father's death. The manner in which his father passed away entailed a prolonged process. It wasn't sudden or violently traumatic, allowing Henry to deal with it over time. The symptoms of grief and PTSD have noteworthy similarities. Both are marked by persistent thoughts of loss, often associated with the death of a loved one, and depression onset from "activities associated with that person, but grief responses are usually worked through with time."[6] Henry could process the mortality of his father gradually over time. It's more likely that he experienced a grief response normal for someone his age.

At eight years old, Henry was old enough to understand his father was gone forever, although his young age did put him at a higher risk for PTSD, even later in life. "Children under the age of 11 are more vulnerable to developing PTSD" because they cannot fully articulate their emotions, and "PTSD can develop years after an event," as has been noted in studies of war veterans.[7] Losing someone that close at such a young age undoubtedly has a profound impact on the emotions and psyche of a developing child. So the question of the influence of his father's death becomes: "Was this the beginning of his PTSD, or was it a precursor to a weakened mental constitution, allowing PTSD to take a stronger hold later?"

At the opposite end of the spectrum was Henry's brother, Jared Lawrence, an infant at the time of their father's death. Jared never knew his biological father, thus he never knew the loss of connection, the grief, or the lost moments. Henry, however, was at a very formative age, just starting to understand the world enough to question its mysteries. He was aware of the respect commanded by his father in Albany, and he watched as hundreds of citizens came to pay their respects at the funeral. Both at home and the funeral service, the grieving process would have been prolonged and cathartic. Henry would have witnessed his mother's reaction, possibly seeing her cry, and these images can take a toll on a young mind. The figures he normally looked to for answers and strength had changed.

The body and mind store these moments, using them as building blocks in a person's foundation. Children log and compile the events they witness. They watch how others operate in the world, learning how to deal with situations by watching those around them and mimicking their actions. Firsthand involvement makes the experience even more visceral. Over time these building blocks are cemented into their personality and mental state as learned traits, blending into the core of who they are.

The death of Jared Lewis Rathbone was the first knock to Henry's psyche. On its own, the event is a formidable misfortune, but less than devastating. The boy would grapple with his father's death and become accustomed to the vacancy it presented in his life. In time, he would adjust accordingly. In the 1800s, death was much more prevalent than it is today. Disease and accidents challenged the medicine of the time, and the passing of family members, especially those in younger stages of life, was relatively typical.

Abraham Lincoln also lost a parent when he was around the same age as Henry. The future President was only nine when his mother passed away from milk sickness. However, Lincoln's experience with burial and the grieving process was far different. Rathbone's father was laid to rest in a tomb fit for Roman nobility whereas Lincoln's mother was buried in a plank wood coffin that Abraham had helped build. According to Carl Sandburg's *Abraham Lincoln: The Prairie Years and War Years*, "Little Abe, with a jack-knife, whittled pine-wood pegs" and held them as his father pounded them into bored holes, holding the planks of his mother's coffin together.

It's hard to accurately determine if the death of Henry's father was a trigger of post-traumatic stress. Because of the lack of medical history on Rathbone, the best we can do is make educated assumptions. Every person reacts differently to trauma. What is a withering blow for one person may cause scarcely a mental ruffle for another. Some individuals are genetically predisposed to post-traumatic stress disorder. Because Henry had delusions of persecution later in life, it's difficult to know whether or not he had a predisposition to paranoid thoughts. He may have had difficulty managing feelings of anxiety even as a child. His father's death may have precipitated a nightmare of emotions for him, but he was able to hide away in a large house with little else to worry about. An affluent upbringing provided Henry the means to escape.

Rathbone's station in life rarely forced a need to overcome hardship, and it's possible that an underlying mental illness was present all along. His prosperous childhood provided a nearly stress-free environment. With servants handling his every need, a successful father, doting mother, and large home in the center of a bustling town, Henry rarely felt the cold hand of an unscrupulous world upon his neck.

Comparing the deaths of Rathbone's father and Lincoln's mother highlights the vastly different experiences that shaped these young boys. Examining how young Henry and young

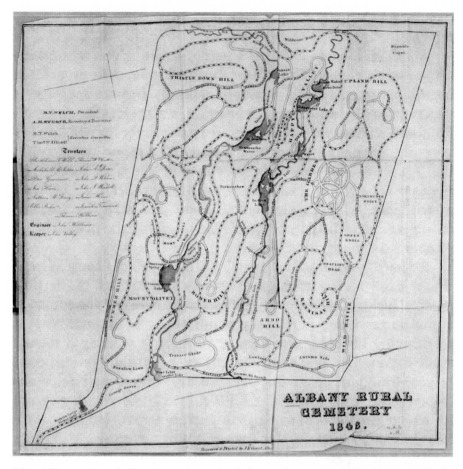

The Albany Rural Cemetery is one of the major cemeteries in New York. The cemetery currently is the last resting place of President Chester A. Arthur, as well as 5 Governors, 3 members of the Continental Congress, 2 members of the Philadelphia Constitutional Convention, 13 members of the Colonial Assembly, 8 Presidential Cabinet members, 5 Ambassadors and many Senators, Congressmen, and Judges.

It also holds the remains of many of the Rathbone and Harris families, Mayor Jared Lewis Rathbone, Pauline and Senator Ira Harris.

The only major exceptions to the family burial grounds are Henry and Clara. Due to their deaths occurring in Hanover, Germany, their bodies were not transported back to New York. After non-payment of cemetery fees and forgotten by family members their remains were later buried deeper to allow new coffins to be placed. Their headstone was removed.

Abraham dealt with their misfortunes presents a remarkable insight into what molds a person's mind. While Henry was an observer of his father's death, Abraham was an actual cog in the process of his mother's. Abraham was forced to face the finality of his mother's existence by helping to put her in the ground in a field amongst a few friends. Henry watched the leaders of Albany pay their respects, both genuine and patronizing, and then walked through one of the largest cemeteries in the state of New York, a cemetery his father helped create.

The death of a parent cannot be trivialized. It was a hardship for both boys, felt equally in their hearts. Henry, though, was cushioned by society, money, and a wealth of free time that allowed his thoughts to dwell. Abraham was forced to move on with his life in order to survive to the next week. He had chores and daily work that required his attention. There was no time for Lincoln to dwell on the loss of his mother.

In an eerily convenient turn of events, three days after the death of Jared Lewis Rathbone, the wife of Ira Harris died. Ira Harris was a local politician and the father of Henry's future wife, Clara Harris. On May 18, 1845, Louisa Tubbs Harris passed away and her body was laid to rest in the Albany Rural Cemetery, not far from Jared Lewis Rathbone. Louisa shared a family burial site with Ira Harris' first wife, who happened to be Louisa's older sister, Clarissa Tubbs Harris.[8] The burial plot also held Clarissa and Ira's infant child Frederick, who passed away at three months of age in 1830.

Despite the bleak and depressing overtones, the timing of Jared Lewis' and Louisa Tubbs' deaths was advantageous to the ambitious Ira Harris, seeing as he would marry Pauline Rathbone, Jared's widow, three years later. Marrying Pauline Rathbone would not only give him an acceptable mother for his four young children, but put him in a great physical location to continue his political career. As mentioned earlier, the Rathbone home sat directly in the center of the capital city. An Eagle Street residence that was a stone's throw from the state Capitol building would provide Ira Harris with easy means to entertain political allies or keep an eye on his adversaries.

Ira Harris (1802 - 1875)
U.S. Senator from New York (1861-1867)
Stepfather to Henry Rathbone and Father of Clara Harris.
Source: National Archives - Mathew Brady Photographs of Civil War-Era Personalities

At the time of Louisa and Jared Rathbone's passing in 1845, Ira Harris was an eager assemblyman for the county of Albany, NY. In fact, the session of the 68th legislature had just ended on May 14, 1845, four days prior to Louisa's death.[9] As a Whig assemblyman, Harris quickly became a vocal part of the 68th New York legislature. He was always one to plan far ahead and map out the quickest route to success. Having laid down the needed foundation of education and experience as a lawyer, he dreamed of playing a prominent role in society. Ira Harris made sure to exact any advantage from every opportunity "to urge him forward in his onward and upward career to fame and fortune. His careful preparation of authorities, his honesty of purpose, his chasteness of language, and his oratorical powers, were well calculated to make him successful."[10]

It's difficult to say how long Ira Harris and Pauline Rathbone may have known each other prior to becoming romantically involved, but it can be reasonably assumed they were at least familiar with each other. With Harris and Jared Lewis Rathbone both actively involved in the city's growth and activities, the two worked together on many projects, such as being trustees of Albany Medical College and both involved in creating the Albany Rural Cemetery. Ira and Pauline also buried their significant others only days apart in the same cemetery. It's quite certain they were aware of each other's station at the time.

On August 1, 1848, three years after their spouses passed away, Ira and Pauline became husband and wife. At the time of the marriage, Ira had become a New York State Supreme Court Judge. The new couple chose to move the two separate families under one roof at the 28 Eagle Street house,[11] bringing the combined total of household members to eight. Harris had four children at the time, three daughters and a son. At thirteen, Clara Harris was the oldest. Henry was eleven, nearly the same age as his new stepbrother, William Hamilton Harris.

With the arrival of Ira Harris, Henry was no longer the man of the house. On top of this, he now had to share his mother's attention not just with his brother, Jared Lawrence, but with another brother and three sisters. Having young girls in the

Henry Rathbone at Union College - 1854
Source: Rathbone Family Historian, Volume Eight, Number Three

house was probably an adjustment for eleven-year-old Henry. Entering the first years of puberty with an influx of same-age females presents a handful for any young boy. His main concern, however, was his new stepfather. Ira Harris "was of commanding personal appearance, being about six feet two inches high, with broad shoulders and a finely developed head. His forehead was broad and high, eyes of a light brown color, large and finely molded nose and mouth and smoothly shaven face. He wore his hair quite long, and generally falling over his forehead. He was graceful in air his movements. As a jurist be was noted for the clearness and ability of his decision. He was a logical reasoner and a ready debater. He was among the best speakers in the Legislature while a member, and rarely failed to fill the chamber when it was given out that he would speak."[12]

Pauline Rathbone's marriage to Judge Harris was probably a little confusing for all of the children involved. Clara and her sister Amanda were the oldest, thirteen and twelve, followed by Henry and William, eleven and ten, and then there was Louise and Jared Lawrence at eight and four, respectively.[13] All of them were old enough to have a routine they were accustomed to, a set way they liked things to be. They were old enough to remember a life with their now deceased parents, making the transition to their new life more difficult. In 1850, Mr. and Mrs. Harris added one more to the brood with the birth of their daughter Pauline. So with the four live-in Irish servants, the Harris household was probably a spirited one. Henry and Clara, however, would not be home much longer. They were both reaching the age where their education would take them away from home completely.

Henry would leave to attend Marlborough Churchill's Military School in Sing-Sing (now Ossining), New York.[14] There are no records of precisely when he attended the military school, but it was a popular choice of school for young men in the New York and surrounding area. Henry's trips home would have been rare during the school year, as it was 120 miles from Albany, but it's logical he would have seen his family during the holidays. Clara would have been home at that time as well, allowing the future couple to become acquainted with each other.

Union College Schenectady, N.Y.
Source: Library of Congress

On April 29, 1854, Henry began his college career at the age of 16, entering Union College in nearby Schenectady, NY.[15] His attendance at Union College was undoubtedly influenced by his stepfather, as he was a trustee of the college and it was his alma mater. Henry was an average student and was enrolled in the classical course schedule with his sights set on a Bachelor of Arts degree. His course schedule was comprised of Latin and Greek, rhetoric, some physics, mental and moral philosophy, criticism, law, chemistry, ·and physiology, and mathematics through "conics" or analytic geometry.[16] Henry was also involved in social activities, becoming a member of the Sigma Phi fraternity. As for Henry's devotion to his education, his record shows that he "frequently missed recitations and, even more frequently, prayers."[17] It's hard to hold this against Henry, though, as it seems common behavior for many boys his age.

Living on-campus, in the North College dormitory, gave Henry a little more freedom than he was probably afforded at home and at military school. His noticeable absence at prayer does bring up the question of his spirituality. Growing up in a Baptist home, under both Rathbone and Harris paternity, provided Henry with a very strict interpretation of religion. The Harris family went to the Pearl Street Baptist Church (later known as Emmanuel Baptist Church), where the family attended the sermons of Pastors Luther F. Beecher and William Hague.[18] The family's attendance at church is noted, however, that does not reflect on the veracity of Henry's commitment to religion. It doesn't appear from the information that Henry was overtly religious, but being that he would grow into a relatively private man it could have been that he kept those feelings and thoughts to himself, even in his youth.

In 1857, after three years of study, Henry graduated from Union College. Upon graduation Henry decided to continue his education and go into the practice of law. He approached his step-uncle, Hamilton Harris, who "had a good practice" at the time and asked him if he "would take him as a law student." Uncle Harris was a bit surprised by this as Henry "was rich, worth about $200,000, but he desired to work and learn a profession." So Harris "gave him a seat by" his "side, and there [Henry] worked hard at law books for a year and a half."[20] Records show that he was admitted to the bar in 1859 and was listed as a "Counsellor at Law" around this time, but that he was not in active practice due to him traveling through Europe.[21] Henry also continued his education at Union College, and in 1860 he received a Master of Arts degree.[22]

4

MILITARY LIFE AND THE CIVIL WAR

Henry Rathbone was extremely busy in his early twenties. His education was on track and he was well on his way to a career in law, but a desire to serve in the military simmered inside him. Despite his general education background and his work at the law office of Hamilton Harris, the patriotic fiber that ran through many men of that era may have been what compelled Henry to enlist in the New York National Guard in 1858. Enlisting also may have been strongly suggested to him by Ira Harris. Whatever the reason, Henry's early time in the state militia helped prepare him for the fast approaching Civil War. Initially serving as Judge Advocate in the National Guard, Henry went on to serve two years as Colonel and Aide-de-Camp on the staff of New York Governor Edwin D. Morgan.[1,2] Working alongside Rathbone as aide-de-camps were E.G. Thompson and Charles W. Darling, all three sharing duties as assistants or secretary to the Governor.

A year later, in 1859, when Sardinia and France declared war on Austria in what was to be known as the Second Italian War of Independence, Rathbone was sent to observe the European armies to further his military knowledge and report back on the activities. These experiences with the National Guard

Henry Rathbone's 1859 Passport application.
Source: National Archives

gave Henry opportunities he wouldn't have received staying in the United States or New York. They did much to advance Henry's life and no doubt helped him grow personally and professionally. His overseas experience also may have been the spark that would ignite his desire to travel and live in Europe later in life.

In 1860, as Henry fulfilled his duties abroad and blazed a path in the military, Abraham Lincoln was embarking on his campaign for the Presidency of the United States. The Rail Splitter gained steam slowly amongst the northern states, as he fought long and hard against his main rival, Democratic candidate Stephen A. Douglas. On November 6, 1860, Abraham Lincoln won the election for the President, running as the Republican Party candidate. Beating out Douglas and Southern candidates John C. Breckinridge and John Bell, Lincoln's election virtually guaranteed Southern secession from the Union. The South had been warning of secession for months, declaring that if Lincoln was elected they would have no representation. In fact, Abraham Lincoln's name wasn't even on the voting ballot in ten southern states, and unlike Stephen Douglas, he never campaigned in the South. So the South saw Lincoln's election as an immediate detriment to their way of life and form of economy. The first seven states, which made up the majority of the Confederacy, seceded from the Union before Lincoln's Inauguration on March 4, 1861.

Henry Rathbone's location cannot be pinpointed during this time. He still may have been traveling through Europe, as Hamilton Harris stated "in 1860 he went to Europe, and travelled about the Continent until the war of the Rebellion broke out," however it's difficult to determine a precise date for Henry's return to the U.S.. But lack of knowledge doesn't prevent stories from being conjured up through hearsay. False facts have a way of filling holes that cannot otherwise be filled, as some people so fear the unknown that loose connections have a way of turning into cold, hard facts. These concoctions become increasingly difficult to disprove with the aid of time and the strength of word of mouth.

A luminous example of historical inaccuracy is the tale of Clara Harris, Henry Rathbone, Abraham Lincoln, and Mary Todd Lincoln all enjoying the thespian talents of Mr. John Wilkes Booth at a play in Albany four years before the assassination. As the legend goes, Booth was performing as Pescara in *The Apostate*, at Albany's Gayety Theatre. Meanwhile, Abraham

GAYETY THEATRE.

J. R. SPACKMAN ....Manager.

Re-appearance of the Great tragedian,
Mr. J. WILKES BOOTH.
This evening will be performed
THE APOSTATE.

Pescara ....Mr. Booth.
DANCE.........................Miss KINCADE.
To conclude with
BOOTS AT THE SWAN.
PRICES OF ADMISSION.
First Tier and Parquette..............80 cents.
Second Tier 25
Private Boxes $5 00
Doors open at 7 ; to commence at 7½ precisely.

Gayety Theatre Ad for *The Apostate*, featuring John Wilkes Booth.

Lincoln's inaugural train was making its way through major cities in New York. During this trip Lincoln meets and greets with citizens, showing his gratitude on his way to Washington to take the Presidential oath of office. The trains stop in Albany allowed the Lincolns to partake in a respite and enjoy a relaxing evening at the Gayety Theater with Judge Ira Harris, who happened to have brought along his daughter Clara Harris and his stepson Henry Rathbone. This tale accounts for every person in the Presidential Box at Ford's Theatre on assassination night 1865.

This story is quite the amazing coincidence and adds yet another layer of mystery to the Lincoln assassination. The problem is it's not true. The basic facts are true. J.W. Booth was performing at the Gayety Theatre and Lincoln was in Albany that same night. But Lincoln's schedule on February 18, 1861, proves that the President-elect was far too busy to have gone to the theater. After a long day of meetings and speeches, Lincoln was the guest of honor at the Governor's mansion for dinner. Afterwards he returned to his room at the Delavan House, where he immediately received visits from the citizens of Albany. *The Morning Courier* and *New York Enquirer* reported that the "Delavan House was crowded to suffocation during the entire evening."[3] The doors of the Gayety Theatre opened at 7:00, and the show started thirty minutes after that. Putting historical trust in the newspapers of the day, it becomes impossible for Lincoln to have attended that evening's performance of *The Apostate*. While Lincoln and Booth may have been in extremely close proximity, and Booth might have watched Lincoln ride into town in the carriage earlier that afternoon, possibly watching the President-elect speak from the Capitol steps, he could not have seen him in the audience at the Gayety Theatre. There's no evidence that Henry Rathbone was in Albany during this time either, in fact he may have still been in Europe. However, three months later, May 1861, he enlisted into the 12th U.S. Infantry. Regardless, if Henry had been in town, he and Lincoln did not cross paths with Booth at the Gayety.

Upon Henry's enlistment in the 12th U.S. Infantry, he was immediately commissioned the rank of Captain. Now twenty-four, Henry was an Officer in the Army and leading a well-respected life. Looking ahead—and keeping his struggle with mental illness in mind—this serves as an important turning point in Henry's life. Up to now, he'd encountered very little adversity. Other than the death of his father, most things had been handed to him or had come his way relatively easily. As Hamilton Harris noted, Henry was not lacking in any fiduciary sense, and Rathbone obtained occupation so easily that many wondered if his relation to Ira Harris played any part in his easy wins. The political game was nothing new to Ira, and he was not afraid to ask for favors. With the war beginning, all was about to change, both for Henry and for the nation.

By this time Ira Harris was the newly elected Senator of New York. It was 1861, and upon William Seward being selected as Abraham Lincoln's Secretary of State, Judge Harris was chosen to fill the open seat. Harris would have had great difficulty winning the election on his own. But he was selected by William Seward and newspaper publisher Thurlow Weed, and with considerable help from the political machine created by these two men, he won the spot.

With Ira Harris' term beginning in March 1861, it was decided that the entire family would make the move to Washington, D.C., including Clara. The family moved to a large house on the corner of H and 15th Street, only a couple blocks from the White House, and quickly associated with the well-connected and affluent people in town. The family was well regarded in capital city society, and Ira, Pauline, and Clara Harris became close friends with Abraham and Mary Todd Lincoln. Ira was such a close acquaintance of Abraham Lincoln that according to Lincoln biographer Benjamin Thomas, Senator Harris was among President Lincoln's "most frequent evening visitors."[4] In fact, Harris' visits were so frequent that Lincoln once claimed that he looked under his bed each night to check if Senator Harris were there, seeking another patronage favor.[5]

It wasn't just the President that Senator Harris formed a strong bond with. He was also very close with Mary Todd Lincoln. In a letter dated March 23, 1865, nearing the end of a congressional session, Mrs. Lincoln wrote to Charles Sumner that "Judge Harris called last evening to say, farewell. He has been so kind a friend that I am quite as attached to him as if he were a relative."[6]

It was these relationships that drew the Lincoln, Harris, and Rathbone families together. Not only were they political allies, but they enjoyed one another's company in social settings. Pauline and Clara Harris were also close friends of Mary Todd and were frequent guests of Mrs. Lincoln to theater outings, parties, and other social gatherings.

One of the first requests that Ira Harris made to President Lincoln was to have Henry's younger brother, Jared Lawrence Rathbone, appointed a cadetship at West Point Military Academy. Lincoln politely obliged, and in a letter to Secretary of War Simon Cameron dated May 27, 1861, the President asked, "If there be any vacancy" he wished to appoint Jared, "provided he fills the conditions."[7] Jared Lawrence was admitted to West Point that same year.[8]

Ira Harris wasn't just asking favors of powerful friends, he was putting his own name and power to use as well. To show his support of the war, Harris helped to create the Fifth New York Cavalry. The regiment, which was authorized on July 26, 1861, was named "in honor of Senator Ira Harris", "under whose patronage the organization was commenced and completed."[9]

Henry Reed Rathbone (1837 - 1911)
Source: National Archives

As Ira began his term as Senator and Jared Lawrence prepared for West Point, Henry was busy on recruiting duty for the Union. He did this for nearly a full year, until March 1862. Assigned to Fort Hamilton in Brooklyn's New York Harbor, Henry's job was to assist in building and organizing his company.[10] This was his first duty in the Civil War, and it provided him the opportunity to generate contacts and friendships with fellow soldiers. He learned the organization of the Army and relied on the Rathbone trait of building something from the ground up.

That said, recruiting men into the war wasn't a difficult task in 1861. Men were raring to go and fight for their respective sides. As Diane Miller Sommerville stated in her article *A Burden Too Heavy to Bear*, "The 'Boys of '61' were pulled into military service by *rage militaire*, a sense of adventure, but they were also pushed into service by patriotic womenfolk who, despite reservations, implored their husbands and sons to enlist. To resist would raise questions about one's manhood as well as commitment to nation." It was this excitement and social stigma at the beginning of the Civil War that made Henry's job a little easier. The official date of organization for the 12th Infantry was October 20, 1861, although the regiment didn't leave New York until March 5, 1862.

Up to this point in the war, Henry hadn't seen any action in battle, but this would soon change when in March the 12th Infantry regiment joined the Army of the Potomac. Henry's battalion was assigned to the infantry reserves, under Brigadier General George Sykes. At the time, the entire Army of the Potomac was under the command of Major General George B. McClellan. The first move Henry and his regiment made took them from New York to Washington, D.C., where they received orders to move to the Virginia peninsula soon after their arrival. Their first combat experience was at the Siege of Yorktown on April 5, 1862. The Yorktown battle was a part of the Peninsula Campaign, a series of battles from March to July 1862, which had the goal of capturing the Confederate capital of Richmond.

For the Union soldiers of the 12th Infantry and many others, it was their first ever contact with Confederate soldiers. The total casualties at Yorktown were 482. Three hundred of those casualties were Confederates. The "enthusiasm and rejoicing" that permeated through the 12th infantry upon them joining the Army of the Potomac was undoubtedly dwindling. The realities of war now stared the soldiers straight on and it was only the beginning.

The battles that followed Yorktown are known now as the Seven Days Battles. From June 25 to July 1, the Army of the Potomac engaged in six major battles with Robert E. Lee's Confederate soldiers. The battles were part of the end of the Peninsula Campaign, which started with Yorktown and ultimately saw Lee push the Union army away from their intended goal of Richmond, Virginia. The Seven Days Battles amounted to heavy casualties for each side and included battles in Mechanicsville, Gaines Mill, Turkey Bridge, and Malvern Hill. In total, approximately 36,000 casualties were estimated for both sides, 16,000 in the Union Army and 20,000 among the Confederates.[11]

As the casualties added up around him, Henry's own bodily health started to suffer. He was sick for two months that summer with fever,[12] but it's not clear whether or not he missed any battles. During this same time, the 12th Infantry became a part of General Pope's Northern Virginia Campaign and was heavily involved in the battles of Groverton and Bull Run in late August 1862.

In September, they joined General McClellan in the Maryland Campaign, just in time for the Battle of Antietam, the bloodiest one-day battle in United States history.[13] The casualties at Antietam, which included those killed, wounded, and missing, totaled approximately 22,000.

On September 16, Rathbone and the 12th Infantry, now attached to the 5th Army Corps, relieved the 4th Infantry near sunset at the Middle Bridge crossing over the Antietam creek.[14] While the majority of the battle took place a few miles away on the Lower Bridge, also known as Burnside's Bridge, the soldiers guarding the Middle Bridge faced some adversity and had casualties as well. According to the report of Captain Matthew M. Blunt, the 12th Infantry "was ordered to relieve the 4th Infantry in guarding the bridge over Antietam Creek, which it did until about 12 p.m. on the following day (17th), when the tide of battle

President Lincoln at the Antietam Battlefield, October 3, 1862. Lincoln is facing General McClellan with other Union Army officers grouped outside the tent.
Source: Library of Congress

uncovering the country on the other side of the bridge," and the horse artillery and cavalry "crossed the bridge at a gallop. The enemy opened a very heavy fire of artillery and cavalry crossing the bridge, from which" the 12th Infantry lost one wounded. "The sharpshooters of the enemy annoying Captain Tidball's battery" and General Pleasonton asked Blunt to "advance a line of skirmishers to drive them back, which was immediately done under command of Captain Winthrop. Shortly after, General Sykes ordered the battalion to advance as a support of Tidballs' battery. This was done, skirmishers being thrown out to the left of the battery."

After this Captain Blunt received no further orders during the rest of the afternoon, and remained in the position assigned until ordered to join the brigade at about 7:00 p.m. The final tally of 12th Infantry losses was 1 killed and 3 wounded. In the report

Middle Bridge or Orndorff Bridge over Antietam Creek (pre-Civil War).
Source: Library of Congress

Captain Blunt specifically names Capt. H.R. Rathbone as acting field officer, commanding Company C.[15]

Despite the major loss of life and a few missteps taken by the Union army, the Battle of Antietam proved successful enough for Abraham Lincoln to use it to justify an act that would have reverberations throughout world history. The Emancipation Proclamation was an executive order declaring freedom for all slaves living in the ten Confederate states, and the President had been waiting for a decisive enough Union victory before issuing it. Lincoln needed to link it to a victory to make it clear that the emancipation of slaves was seen as a move of strength and power, not an act of desperation. Antietam entailed a major political win for the Union, especially internationally. At the time the Confederacy had been pushing for recognition and assistance from powerful countries overseas, particularly Britain and France. After the Battle of Antietam and the Emancipation Proclamation, popular opinion swayed to the Union side.

Following Antietam, Henry remained with his battalion through several more battles through the end of 1862. His last battle of the year, after a long trip north to Falmouth, VA, was the Battle of Fredericksburg on December 12. The battle lasted approximately four days and is widely regarded as a major loss for the Union army. The estimated casualties for the Union forces far surpassed those of the Confederates, at 13,353 to 4,576, respectively.[16]

After his return from the Battle of Fredericksburg, Henry remained in Washington, D.C. for a little over a year. From February 1863 until March 1864 he worked in the Commissary of Musters on the staff of recently appointed Military Governor of the District of Columbia John H. Martindale. His job duties are unclear, and typically his occupation is listed as "special duty," although the office most likely dealt with monies and paperwork necessary for a specific regiment, in this case the military district of Washington, D.C.

It's also not quite certain how Henry obtained this position. After almost a year in battle with the 12th Infantry, he was now behind a desk, able to be a part of society again. It's possible that the toll taken by the war was wearing on his mind, possibly even his body. Henry became ill again in the winter of 1863, continuing into the initial months of 1864. This time the symptoms were malaria-like.[17] Regardless of the reason, Henry clearly needed the time away from the battlefield. Despite the lack of evidence that Henry was ever engaged in major combat himself, seeing firsthand the tragedies of war and being surrounded by death seemed to eat away at him.

Henry's battlefield hiatus also provided an opportunity for the young soldier to become better acquainted with his stepsister Clara. At this point in their lives Henry was twenty-six and Clara was twenty-nine. The two, of course, knew each other from their time in Albany, but so much had happened since then. Henry had graduated from college, traveled through Europe, and seen the horrors of war. Clara was now a grown woman and completely indoctrinated in the trappings of Washington life. She undoubtedly had tales and gossip to share with Henry. They were given time to grow as a couple and appreciate each other not only as step-siblings, but as possible lovers. This time away from the war allowed the seeds of a relationship to be sewn, and Henry came to understand more intimately how fleeting life could be. After watching the men he commanded perish and seeing the lifeless bodies of his fellow soldiers, it's possible that, fueled by an appreciation for the fragility of life, he summoned the courage to announce feelings for Clara. Feelings that may have been simmering in him for years.

Henry's time home was short-lived, however, and in the spring of 1864 he became the Acting Aide-de-Camp to General Ambrose Burnside, Army of the Potomac. Henry held this position for the remainder of his time in battle and he participated in the Rapidan Campaign, which involved the Battles of Wilderness, Spotsylvania, North Anna, and Cold Harbor. It was due to his participation in the Rapidan Campaign that he later received his Major by Brevet on August 1, 1864, for gallant and meritorious service.

The next month, in September 1864, Henry was given a special assignment by President Lincoln. There was a prison in Rock

Island, Illinois that held Confederate prisoners of war. Lincoln intended to convert these prisoners of war into Union soldiers, even though General Grant didn't approve of this tactic. Under no circumstances, did Grant want southern prisoners allowed to enlist in the northern army. But Lincoln was running low on resources and troops and saw an opportunity to remedy this a little. So Lincoln ordered Henry to travel to Rock Island and recruit any soldiers that were willing to enlist in the Union Army.

Henry traveled to Illinois on September 22 to begin the process. As President Lincoln did throughout the war, he was playing both sides at once. This was part of his political mastery. On the same day he sent Rathbone to Rock island Abraham Lincoln wrote a letter to Grant, explaining the intentions of Rathbone.[18] Lincoln knew the recruitment of Southern soldiers had to be done behind Grant's back.

On October 8, 1864, Henry completed his recruitment and created a list of men who were willing to enlist in the Northern army. Henry was to stay on and supervise the examination and muster of these "Galvanized Yankees," but when General Grant found out what had taken place, he ordered the men be put into one regiment and stationed on border patrol in the West.[19]

After returning from Rock Island, Henry went to work for the Provost-Marshal General Bureau in Washington, D.C. It seemed that life away from the battlefield appealed to Henry, and he was most likely enjoying the extra time with Clara. They were soon to be engaged, if this had not already happened. The exact date is unclear, but the couple was engaged prior to the assassination, which was only six months away.

Henry's first position with the Provost-Marshal General Bureau was as the Commissary of Musters, 1st Army Corps. The work seemed to interest Henry and he did well at his job. In March 1865, he was put in charge of the 1st Division of the Disbursing branch, which was charged with the disbursement of all funds for collecting, drilling, and organizing volunteers for the war. It also oversaw all the funds for enrollment, drafting, and raising troops. The disbursing office verified the expenses related to these duties and determined if payment was to be made.[20] This promotion saw him gain a commission as an officer in the U.S. Volunteers Adjutant General Department of Infantry Regiment. On the same day, he obtained his Full Major status, giving him the title of Major Rathbone.

By April 1865, all seemed to be going well for Henry and Clara. Henry had a well-paying job and a secure future in the military. He was being promoted and recognized, and had been away from the battlefield for nearly a year. Their high spirits must have matched the atmosphere permeating the North at that time, especially in Washington, D.C. On April 9, 1865, General Robert E. Lee surrendered the Army of Northern Virginia, signaling the end of the war was very close.

In addition to the jubilant news on the national front, the young couple was engaged to be married and enjoyed life as popular guests in society. Their relationship was blossoming and were now able to spend more time with one another. When not in each other's company, however, Clara and Henry maintained their separate lives.

As discussed earlier, Clara was a dear friend of Mary Todd Lincoln and joined her on many occasions. In fact, Clara was invited to the White House on Tuesday April 11, 1865, for a speech Abraham Lincoln delivered from an open window. A speech that John Wilkes Booth watched as part of the crowd outside. It was two days after Lee's surrender at Appomattox and three days before Lincoln's assassination.

5
APRIL 14, 1865

Investigating the details of Lincoln's last day can easily evolve into a game of "he said, she said." For over a century, the facts of the assassination day have been argued by experts, with new evidence sporadically coming to light. Additionally, if the status quo becomes stale and there's even the slightest bit of wiggle room, novel interpretations of old evidence can gain new followers.

The assassination of Abraham Lincoln was a major turning point for the United States, and for Henry Rathbone it was the linchpin to his sanity. To properly understand the effect that night's events had on Henry and Clara's lives, we must probe the various possible scenarios. The standard version of the events provides a solid foundation from which to start. From there, delving into the foggy details will uncover what else may have happened that night. Bringing to bear all the available information gives the investigation into Henry's life a better backbone and may shed new light on the emotional devastation it wrought on him.

Henry and Clara's invitation to Ford's Theatre didn't arrive until approximately six o'clock on April 14, 1865. The exact time is not known, but up until that time prior engagements were being made by the President and his wife. Henry and Clara, along with most of the city, were probably aware the Lincolns planned on attending the play, *Our American Cousin*, later that night. It was to be Laura Keene's final performance of the role she'd originated in 1858.

The attendance of President Lincoln was announced in the daily newspapers, the *Washington Evening Star* and the *National*

LIEUT. GENERAL GRANT, PRESIDENT and Mrs. Lincoln have secured the State Box at Ford's Theater TO NIGHT, to witness Miss Laura Keene's American Cousin.   It

DAWSON LODGE. No. 16.—There will be a called meeting of Dawson Lodge, No. 16, held on SATURDAY AFTERNOON, April 15, at 3 o'clock. All Master Masons are fraternally invited to be present. By order of the W. M.
ap 14 2t*   G. R. THOMPSON, Secretary.

MASONIC.—A special meeting of LEBANON LODGE, No. 7, F. A. M., will be held on SATURDAY EVENING, 15th inst., at 7½ o'clock, at Central Masonic Hall, corner of 9th and D streets. All Master Masons are invited to be present. By order of the W. M
ap 14-2t*   C. W. DARR, Secretary.

THE REGULAR MONTHLY MEETING of the Board of Managers of the Young Men's Christian Association will be held at their rooms, No 500 7th street, THIS (Friday) EVENING, at 7½ o'clock.
The new Board will also assemble at the same hour.   WARREN CHOATE,
It   Recording Secretary.

LIEUT GENERAL GRANT, ARRIVED in town last evening, on his way to Philadelphia will visit Ford's Theater THIS EVENING, in company with President and Mrs. Lincoln.
It

From the *Evening Star* newspaper, April,14 1865, page 2.
The top and bottom announcements state the attendance of the President, Mary Todd Lincoln and General Grant.
Source: Library of Congress

Intelligencer, and word was spreading quickly around the capital. The advertisement in the paper, however, also mentioned that General Ulysses S. Grant and his wife, Julia, were to be guests of the Lincolns, accompanying them in the Presidential box. The managers of Ford's Theatre, James and Harry Ford, were exalted by the news and arranged an impromptu celebration for the arrival of the President and General Grant. The announcement of the famous guests thrilled the Ford's Theatre managers because attendance on Good Friday was normally quite low, so the President and General's arrival was sure to boost ticket sales.[1]

It would provide a rare sight for theater-goers to witness the President and his victorious General side-by-side, enjoying a rousing comedy in the balcony of one of Washington's finest playhouses. The attendance of General Grant was even more exciting than that of Lincoln, as Grant was rarely seen in public, having been engaged in battle for so long.

Arrangements for the Grants were planned days in advance. While Mary Todd and Julia Grant were not on the best of terms, Mary Todd still desired to have the Grants join them. It would have been a great public appearance. The Grant couple, however, had prior plans to visit their children in New Jersey and this was their main priority. The train they planned on taking was scheduled to leave Friday afternoon before the play began. General Grant still had work that required his attention in Washington, and he assumed they would not be able to leave for New Jersey until Saturday. It was with this in mind that Grant initially accepted Lincoln's invitation.

After Lincoln's last cabinet meeting on the assassination day, Grant informed him that he had been able to complete his work and that he and his wife would be leaving for New Jersey after all.[2] They were scheduled to be in Baltimore that night in order to catch a train to Burlington, New Jersey.

It's also believed that Julia's disdain for Mary Todd compelled little deliberation over whether to catch the train or attend the play. Mrs. Lincoln and Mrs. Grant had not been in each other's favor for some time. The feelings dated back to a trip to City Point, Virginia in which Mary Todd lost her temper and insulted

Julia, screaming, "I suppose you think you'll get to the White House yourself, don't you?"[3] Regardless of the reason, the couple politely rescinded their acceptance.

Clara and Henry were not the second choice of the Lincolns. In fact, they were so far down the line that it's possible their invitation was a last ditch effort so that Mary Todd and the President would not show up alone. Arriving without the Grants was sure to be a disappointment for the crowd, but having no guests at all would have been a fit of social embarrassment for Mrs. Lincoln. A constant concern of Mary Todd's was the social standing and public appearance of her and the President. Even before their arrival to Washington she feared the aristocrats of the capital city looking down upon the Lincolns' apparent country lifestyle and background. This fear was enhanced by Mrs. Lincoln's anxiety, but also contained a sliver of truth. The President, however, did not bother himself with such mundane worries.[4]

The list of invitees that declined before the invitation reached Clara and Henry was long and distinguished. The first to be invited following the news that Grant would not be attending was Indiana Representative and soon-to-be seventeenth Vice-President of the United States, Schuyler Colfax. Mr. Colfax politely declined, his reason being that he was leaving for a trip to the West Coast early the next morning.[5] Next, an invitation went out to Noah Brooks, a reporter living in Washington and long-time friend of Lincoln's. Brooks was in town covering Lincoln and his presidency for the *Sacramento Daily Union*. Brooks had to decline the invitation, however, as he was feeling ill that day and informed the President that he was heading home early to fight off a cold.[6]

The Lincoln's oldest son, Robert, was also invited to the play. Robert arrived in Washington that same morning after having come from the surrender of Robert E. Lee in Appomattox, Virginia. At breakfast Robert regaled his father with accounts of General Grant and General Lee. His parents offered a seat for that night's play, but Robert was tired from his trip and was looking forward to getting a good night's rest.

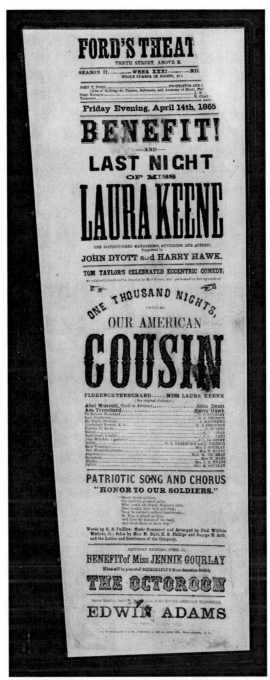

Poster for *Our American Cousin* at Ford's Theatre, starring Laura Keene.
Source: Library of Congress

Mary Todd Lincoln next turned her attention to a visitor from France, the Marquis Adolphe de Chambrun. The Marquis de Chambrun was a diplomat of sorts, sent by France to report back on the progress of the Civil War and President Lincoln. He was quickly accepted by Mary Todd, no doubt due to his title and aristocratic manners. For this reason the Marquis became privy to many personal moments between the President and Mary Todd. In letters to his wife, later compiled into the book, *Impressions of Lincoln and the Civil War*, Marquis de Chambrun made reference to the invitation to Ford's Theatre. The Marquis declined with hesitation, however, stating, "even at the risk of offending White House etiquette" he couldn't "attend a theatrical performance on Good Friday."[7]

Attending the theater on Good Friday may not strike most people today as much of a faux-pas, and to many Americans in 1865 it wasn't much of a transgression either. But as Lincoln's secretary, John Nicolay, mentioned in his book, *A Short Life of Abraham Lincoln*, "It has always been a matter of surprise in Europe that (Lincoln) should have been at a place of amusement on Good Friday; but the day was not kept sacred in America, except by the members of certain churches."[8]

As time ran short, Abraham and Mary Todd took every opportunity to find a replacement for the Grants. Around three o'clock that day at the War Department, Secretary of War Edwin Stanton informed Lincoln with "regrets" that he and his wife would be unable to attend the play with them. Stanton's declination may have been related to his worry that it was not safe for Lincoln to appear at such a public event, and he took the opportunity to remind Lincoln of this warning again. Stanton feared an attack on the President's life and asked Lincoln to reconsider his plans. Also, Stanton's wife Ellen, like Mrs. Grant and many in Washington, was not overly fond of Mary Todd Lincoln.[9]

In hindsight, the reluctance of friends and acquaintances to attend *Our American Cousin* with Lincoln gravitates to the idea that Henry and Clara's participation was predestined. Was Henry fated to be the man in the back of the Presidential box? How might events have turned out differently? If Henry and Clara had not been able to attend, would the Lincolns have attended the theater at all? From the scant accounts of those he interacted with that day, Lincoln wasn't very excited about attending the show either. Normally, Lincoln welcomed a night at the theater, using it as a chance to relax and avoid office seekers for a while. With the war coming to a close, however, Lincoln was in high spirits and had no need of the diversion or camouflage of the theater. He felt it a duty since his arrival had been publicized and their presence was expected. "It has been advertised that we will be there, and I cannot disappoint the people. Otherwise I would not go. I do not want to go," Lincoln mentioned to White House guard William H. Crook that day.[10]

Still concerned about the possibility of an attack, Stanton advised that Lincoln at least bring along a guard. If an attack were planned, Stanton wanted the President to have some kind of protection. Thus, the President proceeded to offer an invitation to the telegraph officer, Thomas Eckert. Lincoln knew Eckert from his many trips to the War Department over the years and started regaling Secretary Stanton with tales of Eckert's strength.

"Stanton, do you know Eckert could break a poker over his arm?" Lincoln said, referring to several fireplace pokers the President had seen Eckert break months before.

He was baiting Stanton, and when the Secretary blindly asked why the President would "ask such a question". Lincoln requested to have Eckert along for protection that night. Outwitted by Lincoln, Stanton quickly countered that Eckert had work to complete at the War Department in the hopes this latest denial would become one more reason for the President not to attend the play. Lincoln didn't accept Secretary Stanton's response and offered the invitation to Eckert in person.

In doing so, the President politely gave Eckert a way out of the invitation, as he divulged the fact that Stanton needed him for work. Eckert found himself in an odd position. A request to attend an event with Abraham Lincoln didn't come often. But as Stanton stood nearby awaiting his response, Eckert advised the President that he had too much work to finish that evening.

Photograph from the last formal portrait sitting, Feb. 5, 1865, in Washington, D.C.
Source: Library of Congress

Mary Todd Lincoln (1818 - 1882)
Source: National Archives

Clara Hamilton Harris (1834 - 1883)
Source: National Archives

Two tickets to Ford's Theatre in the Dress Circle. The Dress Circle was on the same level as the Presidential box. Lincoln and his guests passed through the back of the dress circle on their way to the private box.
Source: National Archives

The carriage that Abraham Lincoln and his guests traveled in to Ford's Theatre. It was built by the Wood Brothers in 1864 an now resides at The Studebaker National Museum.
Source: B.R. Howard and Associates, Inc.

Ford's Theatre is the large building in the middle. The image is dated between the years of 1860-1880 and is a good example of the conditions on 10th street during that time.
Source: Library of Congress

Lincoln was adamant, stating, "You can do Stanton's work tomorrow, and Mrs. Lincoln and I want you with us." Eckert didn't want to upset his boss by overriding the decision already made, however, so he thanked Lincoln again, noting that the work couldn't be put off.[11]

Finally, with all other possibilities nearly exhausted, Clara and Henry received their invitation. With the play only a few hours away the couple undoubtedly realized they were not the first choice, although it's unknown if they were aware of just how far down the list they were.

As the Presidential family ate dinner together that night, Mary Todd informed Abraham that Ms. Harris and Major Rathbone would be joining them at Ford's Theatre. At long last the issue had been resolved. Lincoln met with a few more visitors later that evening, and just after eight o'clock, the President and Mrs. Lincoln exited through the front doors of the White House and got into an awaiting carriage.

The carriage was an open barouche model, built in 1864 by the Wood Brothers, and was a comfort to ride in with six springs and solid silver lamps. As Mary Todd Lincoln approached the

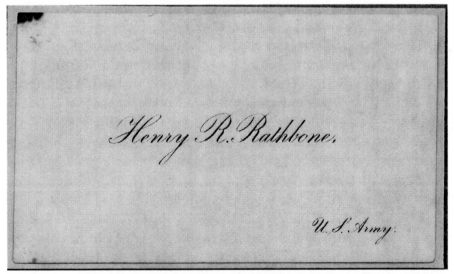

This is Henry R. Rathbone's calling card. This card is similar to the one that John Wilkes Booth handed Charles Forbes, before entering the Presidential box.
Source: National Archives

carriage, the steps, connected to the doors, lowered as the door opened and raised back into hiding once the door was closed. The trip to pick up Clara and Henry was a short one. The couple was waiting at the home of Senator Harris only a few blocks from the White House on the corner of H and 15th Streets.

Clara was a "dark and lovely" thirty years old. A socialite and popular woman in D.C., she was a "full-figured girl with rows of tiny spitcurls on her forehead."[12] Henry at this time was twenty-eight. He was tall for the time period, at five-foot-ten, and slender with a quiet demeanor. The features most notable on Henry were his auburn hair and prominent nose. His small mouth was masked by his "muttonchop whiskers and a walrus mustache,"[13] and he portrayed all the fine qualities of his dignified upbringing.

The President and his wife sat with their backs to the driver, as Clara and Henry entered the coach around eight-twenty, sitting directly across from them. Clara noted that the President and Mary Todd arrived in "the gayest spirits" and that the couples chatted along the way. In the front of the coach sat Francis P. Burke, the coachman, and Charles Forbes, Lincoln's messenger and valet. The trip to Ford's Theatre, on 10th Street, was also short, and at eight-thirty the Lincolns and their guests arrived.

The party was greeted by John M. Buckingham, the Ford's Theatre doorkeeper, and John Parker, an officer of the Metropolitan Police Force who had been assigned as the President's guard for the night. The President rarely enjoyed the company of a guard and had a somewhat cavalier attitude regarding his safety. Due to the ever-growing threats to the President, however, officers were normally assigned protective service.

The Metropolitan police protection was still rather new, as was the entire police force, created in 1861, with the presidential protection program created just five months before the assassination. The Washington police was the first group of officers to guard the President in a revolving detail. Parker, though, was three hours late that night to relieve the guard on duty. Parker's shift was to begin at four o'clock, but he arrived at nearly seven. This wasn't unexpected behavior from John Parker.

Panoramic View of Ford's Theatre. The Presidential box is on the far left and decorated with flags and the portrait of George Washington. The middle floor is the Dress Circle. At the back of the Dress Circle, from right to left, is the path that Abraham Lincoln and his guests took and later John Wilkes Booth.

Source: Library of Congress

Side view of Ford's Theatre, looking across into the Presidential box.
Source: Library of Congress

This view into the Presidential box is similar to what John Wilkes Booth
would have seen when he entered. Lincoln sat in the first seat, then Mary
Todd Lincoln. Henry Rathbone was seated on the couch and Clara next to
him in the far chair.
Source: Library of Congress

John Wilkes Booth. He originally planned on kidnapping Lincoln to assist the South in winning the war.
Source: Library of Congress

This the exact rocking chair that Abraham Lincoln sat in during the performance of *Our American Cousin*. The chair he was shot in.
Source: Library of Congress

He had a reputation as a drunk, using inappropriate language and frequenting brothels. Unfortunately for all involved, Parker was assigned that night's shift and was ordered to meet the President and his guests at Ford's Theatre.[14]

The Presidential party exited the carriage and entered the front doors, opened by Buckingham. Charles Forbes led the way through the theater lobby and up the winding stairs to the second level dress circle. As the group made its way through the back of the dress circle behind the theater-goers, Lincoln's presence was realized by Laura Keene on stage. She stopped the play, and the orchestra broke out into an impromptu performance of "Hail to the Chief." According to Union War Department clerk James Suydam, Lincoln entered the theater "amid deafening cheers and the rising of all...Never was our Magistrate more cheerfully welcomed, or more happy."[15]

The President acknowledged the audience as the party continued on to the Presidential box. The capacity of the theater was approximately 1,700, but it was hard to get an exact number due to bench seating in the family circle, the cheapest seats, going for twenty-five cents. The dress circle seats cost seventy-five cents, whereas the orchestra level on the main floor cost one dollar. The President's State box normally cost ten dollars, and records show there were no other boxes occupied that night.[16]

The dress circle patrons, on the same floor as the President's box, received the best view of Lincoln and his guests. Turning around in their chairs, the audience watched Lincoln and Mary Todd passing by and possibly wondered who it was that accompanied them. It certainly wasn't General Grant and his wife. Reaching the end of the left balcony, Lincoln and his guests passed through the hallway door, entering into the vestibule that led to boxes 7 and 8. The vestibule was approximately four feet wide and ten feet long, consisting of door 7 and door 8. During regular performances at Ford's Theatre, the President's State box was actually two separate boxes, with doors 7 and 8 leading to them. However, on occasions such as the President's attendance, the two boxes were combined into one larger box through the use of a moveable partition.

Abraham Lincoln and his guests entered the combined State box through door 8. Charles Forbes stayed out in the dress circle, sitting as close as possible to the vestibule door, in seat number 300.[17] John Parker took a seat in the vestibule itself, between the two doors separating the box seats and the aisle in the dress circle. How long Parker actually stayed in his guard seat is still a major point of contention among historians. Because of Lincoln's disregard for his personal safety and his distaste for guards hovering around, many believe Lincoln relieved Parker of his duty before taking his seat. There are other theories in which Parker left his seat to watch the play, lacking a view of the stage from inside the vestibule area. Whatever the truth, Parker wasn't there at the moment Booth came to visit that night.

When the Lincolns, Henry Rathbone, and Clara Harris entered the Presidential box they found a black walnut rocking chair close to door 8 and resting nearly in front of door 7. Beside the rocker was a straight-backed cane chair. Lincoln and his wife sat in the rocker and cane chair, respectively. On the far side of the Presidential box was another straight-backed chair, and behind this chair, pressed against the back wall of the box, was a small, red velvet-covered sofa. Clara sat in the third chair, close to Mrs. Lincoln, and Henry sat on the sofa.

In terms of viewing the production, Henry's seat was the least desirable spot in the Presidential box and possibly in the entire theater. In the back of a box that was directly over the stage, Henry would have had difficulty seeing much of the play. He also had to contend with the large pillar in the middle of the box and the railing in front, both of which had curtains and flags draping from them. In short, notwithstanding the impending tragedy, Henry already had the worst seat in the house.

Before President Lincoln finally sat, he took the time to recognize the crowd once more. One person in attendance said that Lincoln "stepped to the box-rail and acknowledged the applause with dignified bows and never-to-be-forgotten smiles."[18] The play was suspended while the crowd continued with its standing ovation, which lasted until the President finally sat down. Once the tardy theater guests had taken their seats, the play commenced, but throughout the night the audience alternated their attention from Laura Keene and Harry Hawk on-stage to President Lincoln in the State box.

Despite the fact that Lincoln was mostly masked by the curtains surrounding the state box, any time the President moved he drew the eye of audience members. Lincoln sat motionless for most of the play, except at one point in which Rathbone notes that Lincoln became cold and got up from his chair to put his coat on. He returned to his seat promptly and continued watching the play in silence. In addition to watching the President's every move, many theater guests in attendance had expected the arrival of General Grant. When Lincoln showed up without him, some assumed Grant would show up late and kept an eye out for him.

Whereas there are numerous accounts of Lincoln's actions and trivial mannerisms that night, the movements of Rathbone are lost. We cannot say if he was intently drawn to the show. We do not know if he doted on Clara, ensuring her comfort or enjoyment. Although Mrs. Lincoln fretted about what "Miss Harris will think of my hanging on to you so?" as she held the President's hand and Abraham responded that Miss Harris wouldn't "think anything about" it, we don't know for sure if Henry and Clara displayed similar affectionate turns.[19]

The actions of John Wilkes Booth, however, are a little better known. Booth heard of Lincoln's intention to visit Ford's Theatre only hours before curtain. Although he already had plans to kill the President, it was believed that Lincoln and his group would be attending Grover's Theatre.

Because of Booth's itinerancy as an actor and his relationship with Ford's Theatre he had his mail delivered there. It was during his customary mail pickup that he first heard the news, when Harry Ford mentioned to him that the President and General would be at that night's performance. Upon hearing this, Booth's mind sprang into action. He hastily revised his assassination plan to Ford's Theatre and contacted the other conspirators: Lewis Powell, George Atzerodt, and David

The Assassination of Abraham Lincoln.
Source: Library of Congress

Herold. The plan was to assassinate the President, the Vice President, and Secretary of State William Seward at the same time. By doing so, they believed they could place the North in such disarray the South could be victorious.

A little after nine o'clock Booth entered the back of Ford's Theatre and demanded Edmund Spangler, a scene shifter and carpenter at the theater, to hold his horse. Spangler accepted only because Booth stormed off without discussion, but soon handed the horse off to Joseph "Peanuts" Burroughs, a theater doorkeeper and stable helper.

Booth made his way underneath the stage. Using a passageway leading out of the theater to Tenth Street, he ordered a whiskey and water at the saloon next door to Ford's. John Wilkes Booth had the plan running through his mind. He was to attack Lincoln as the President was intent on the play. As John Gilmary Shea noted in *The Lincoln Memorial*, Booth had to "strike from behind, for it has been well said, that no one could have looked Abraham Lincoln in the face and done the deed."

Booth had little to worry about. He knew the theater well, having performed there many times and being free to roam the grounds as he pleased. He had his pistol, one shot only, but it was all he'd need. He may have worried that General Grant would attack after hearing the shot, so Booth armed himself with a large hunting dagger in case he had to fend off the war hero.

Leaving the saloon, Booth made his way toward the theater to enter through the lobby. But it was too soon. The entire plan had been coordinated to coincide with Powell's attack on Secretary Seward and George Atzerodt's attack on Vice President Johnson. Booth planned to wait for a particular moment in *Our American Cousin* to make his attack. After asking John Buckingham at the theater door for the time and leaving and re-entering the theater a few times, Booth made his final entrance at ten minutes after ten o'clock.

Walking the same path that the President did earlier in the night, Booth ascended the spiral staircase and headed toward the Presidential box. Charles Forbes, still sitting near the vestibule entrance, was approached by Booth. The assassin handed Forbes a calling card from his pocket, waited a moment, and continued into the vestibule that led to Abraham Lincoln. Whether Forbes expected John Parker to greet him, once inside the vestibule, is not known. Forbes also may have simply expected Booth to greet Lincoln as a visitor.

Inside the Presidential box, as Booth made his entrance just outside, Henry rested a mere seven feet from one of the greatest leaders the world has ever known. Throughout the night, Henry undoubtedly alternated between gazing at the play below to stealing glances of the President. Henry was well versed in the manners of high society, so being in the balcony of a theater was nothing new for him. The play itself was well known, and given Rathbone's unenviable vantage point, his mind no doubt had ample opportunity to wander to thoughts of the President.

Lincoln enjoyed the theater, this was his eighth visit to Ford's since coming to Washington.[20] In fact, Clara had been the theater guest of Mr. and Mrs. Lincoln only one month prior, that time at Grover's Theater. Attending the first performance of Mozart's *The Magic Flute*, Clara was privy that night to a tired and war-torn President. His mood was entirely different from the one he carried this night. A month earlier, Lincoln was so tired that night he could barely keep interest in the play. The other guest that evening, James Grant Wilson, remembered the President noting his weary demeanor by stating, "I have not come for the play, but for the rest. I am hounded to death by office-seekers, who pursue me early and late, and it is simply to get two or three hours' relief that I am here." Then Lincoln closed his eyes.[21]

Henry was not at Grover's that evening for *The Magic Flute*, but Clara probably regaled him with stories about the evening. Informing Henry of the President's tired appearance and disregard for the performance may have given Rathbone validation to act in a similar manner and not pay close attention to the show before him. After all, Rathbone was no doubt weary from a long week, and attending a play on Friday night, Henry may have felt the weight of heavy eyelids as the third act approached.

The Philadelphia Deringer that John Wilkes Booth used to kill Abraham Lincoln. The gun is now on display at the Ford's Theatre museum.

View of the Presidential box from an elevated position from the Ford's Theatre stage. You can see the door Booth entered from behind the rocking chair.
Source: Library of Congress.

Booth was inching closer to his destiny as he silently shut the main door behind him. Holding the door closed, Booth reached over and picked up the wood bar he'd left in the vestibule earlier that day. Lodging it between the main door and the opposite wall, Booth created a barrier behind him, preventing anyone from entering and interfering with his plan.

Booth now had two doors to choose from. Door 7 had a small hole bored completely through to the other side, near the doorknob. Through the hole, Lincoln could be seen from the back resting in the rocking chair. How this hole got there is up for debate. Some claim that Booth or an accomplice bored the hole earlier in the day, providing a vantage point to ascertain the precise location of the President. Frank Ford, son of Harry

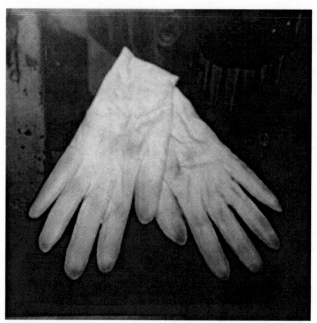

The white gloves that Henry Rathbone wore to Ford's Theatre the night of the assassination. The gloves are on display at the Ford's Theatre museum.

Clay Ford, later stated that his father ordered the hole to be bored into the door. Doing so, he stated, would "allow the guard, one Parker, easy opportunity whenever he so desired to look into the box."[22] Whether or not Booth was connected to the hole, or if it was there already, it did allow viewing into the box.

At that point John Wilkes Booth could have entered the President's box through either door 7 or door 8. Neither was locked, as the locks of both doors had been broken the month before and the doors could be opened by simply pushing on them.[23] Seeing Lincoln through the hole in door 7, however, Booth probably realized the President was practically blocking his path and that entering through door 8 would give him more room to maneuver and possibly a better angle. The only problem now was Henry Rathbone. Then again, Henry may have been a welcome sight to Booth. Like most of the people in attendance that night, he expected General Ulysses S. Grant to be in the box. Instead he found a smaller and less imposing individual wearing civilian clothing.[24]

Henry could still pose a problem, and Booth had little room for error. Henry was directly parallel to door 8, Booth's chosen entrance, and only the darkness of the hallway concealed him from being noticed. In his affidavit, Rathbone stated he didn't notice the door being closed, which meant that Booth had nothing between him and President Lincoln, but could have been noticed immediately upon entering the box. But Henry stated he was "intently observing the proceedings upon the stage with" his "back towards the door."[25]

On stage, the play was nearing one of its pinnacles of humor. *Our American Cousin*, written by Tom Taylor, was one of the biggest hits of the 19th century,[26] and as Booth well knew, the audience's reaction to an upcoming line would provide the perfect cover for his attack. Slowly entering into the President's box, Booth readied his nerves. He was on the precipice of a historical moment. At ten-thirteen, Harry Hawk, playing Asa Trenchard, bellowed out, "Don't know the manners of good society, eh?" John Wilkes Booth moved into position and raised his gun toward the back of Lincoln's head. "Well, I guess I know enough to turn you inside out, old gal – you sockdologizing old mantrap." The crowd erupted into laughter, muffling the report of John Wilkes Booth's pistol.

Those were the last word's Abraham Lincoln heard. John Wilkes Booth took aim quickly and shot true. His single shot Philadelphia Deringer pistol exploded its lead ball directly behind Lincoln's left ear, the ball taking a path "directly forwards through the center of the brain and lodged."[27]

Rathbone "heard the discharge of a pistol" behind him and quickly spun in his seat to find "through the smoke, a man between the door and the President." Henry also stated that he thought Booth shouted the word "Freedom." Although Henry was the only witness to make this claim, he was the closest to Booth at the time and the first person who fully appreciated what had taken place.

Without wasting another moment, Henry "instantly sprang towards" Booth "and seized him," but the assassin "wrested himself from" Henry's "grasp and made a violent thrust" at Henry "with a large knife." Rathbone saw the attack coming

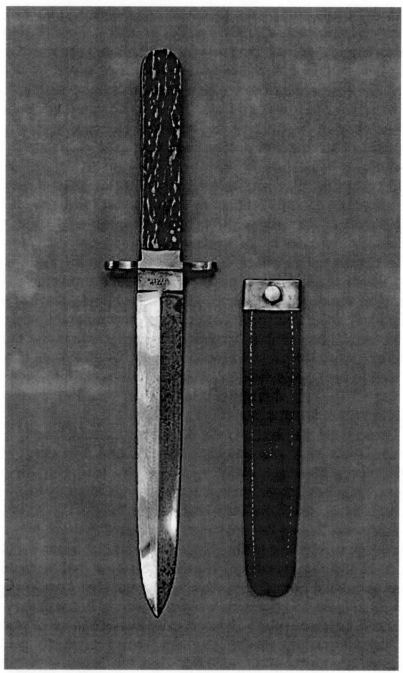

The large hunting dagger that John Wilkes Booth used to injure Henry Rathbone's arm and complete his escape.
Source: National Archives

and "parried the blow by striking it up and received a wound several inches deep in" his "left arm between the elbow and the shoulder."[28] The wound was "about an inch and a half" wide and ran "upwards towards the shoulder several inches."[29]

The grapple between Booth and Rathbone was quick and intense. It was also a moment that Henry had to face alone. There was no one there to help him and no one to share the burden. Confronting the killer of President Abraham Lincoln was something he'd have to bear by himself. It was Henry's opportunity and for the rest of his life, the outcome would only be carried by him.

Were it not for the dagger, Henry may have succeeded in apprehending the assassin. In comparing the two men we see they stacked up very well against one another. They were nearly the same age, Booth being twenty-six and Henry only two years older at twenty-eight. They were nearly the same height as well. Henry stood five-foot-ten whereas Booth was a bit shorter at five-foot-eight. John Wilkes Booth was well known for his athletic bounding on stage, performing great feats of daring, sword fights, and powerful, vigorous movements. While Henry was a trained soldier, his duties as an officer required more skill in leadership than in combat. However according to G.W. Pope, the Harris family doctor, "Rathbone was a man of medium stature and rather slender build, but was possessed of great nerve, power and remarkable physical strength."[30] Alas, while the tale of the tape may have been equal the fight was not. It ended the moment Booth brandished the large dagger and sliced through Henry's upper arm.

With pain pulsing through Henry's arm, he momentarily withdrew from John Wilkes Booth, releasing his grasp. Booth made quick work of the opportunity and "rushed to the front of the box," but Henry recovered quickly. Lunging out, Henry made another attempt to "seize him again but only caught" Booth's clothing as he leapt over the railing of the box. To Henry's recollection, the clothing was torn in this attempt to seize the assassin. The crowd watched in shock as John Wilkes Booth dropped from the balcony and landed upon the stage. Many in the audience later reported that Booth landed awkwardly, possibly injuring himself, maybe even breaking his leg or ankle.

Booth's odd landing may have been due to the unexpected last grasp from Rathbone. Another possibility was the decorations that adorned the outside of the Presidential box. It was decorated with American flags and a framed portrait of George Washington in the center just for that night's performance. According to witnesses, Booth's feet got caught up in these decorations. At the same moment Booth was finding his footing on the edge of the railing, Rathbone made his last attempt at capture. This interference may have been enough to knock Booth off balance, altering his expected path and causing him to sustain an injury.

Injured or not, he rose to his feet, still holding the bloody knife with which he had stabbed Henry, and cried to the crowd, "Sic Semper Tyrannis," meaning "Thus Always to Tyrants," the Virginia state motto. The crowd was still unsure of what was happening and for the most part remained frozen in their seats. Henry broke the silence by yelling out while reaching for Booth in vain, "Stop that man!" Clara quickly echoed the words of her fiancé, yelling, "Stop that man! Won't somebody stop that man?" Booth did not hesitate and quickly escaped through the back doors of the theater, where he mounted the horse being held by "Peanuts" Burroughs. Inside the theater, someone from the stage asked, "What is the matter?" to which Clara cried out, "The President is shot!" It was too late, though. Booth had already ridden off into the night, leaving horror in his wake.

After John Wilkes Booth escaped through the back of Ford's Theatre and news of the attack was announced, the audience went wild. According to witness Captain Oliver Gatch, "the crowd went mad, a wilder night I never saw, not in battle even."[31] Women in the audience were fainting and men began emitting cries of anger. As the fact of what had happened started to sink in, panic was rampant and people began running over one another.

Up in the Presidential box, the scene was deteriorating further. The bleeding from Rathbone's arm continued unabated, and Mary Todd Lincoln began the screams she continued the remainder of the night. Her screams and cries were muffled only by the noise in the theater, and she could do little else but hold

Dr. Charles Leale (1842 - 1932)
Leale was the first doctor to examine Abraham Lincoln after Booth's attack.
Source: Library of Congress

The Petersen House. Owned by William A. Petersen, it was a boarding house directly across the street from Ford's Theatre. Lincoln's body was taken here after the attack.
Source: Library of Congress

the President's head and beseech God for answers. Clara stood by Mary Todd's side trying to console her and provide whatever comfort was possible in the face of such a tragedy.

Henry "turned to the President" and noticed Lincoln's "position was not changed. His head was slightly bent forward and his eyes were closed." Rathbone assumed the worst and concluded the President to be "mortally wounded." However, he knew "medical aid" was needed quickly if Lincoln had even the slightest chance of survival.

He rushed to the main door that led to the dress circle "for the purpose of calling" for a doctor. He could hear the pounding of fists "beating against the door for the purpose of entering" and moved quickly to open it. His first attempt to open the door was futile. The door was "barred by a heavy piece of plank" approximately "four feet from the floor." Henry thrust his weight against it, holding his injured arm against his body. The blood had soaked his sleeve and poured from the large gash, pooling on the ground. Henry's adrenaline had long ago taken over, and with a strong heave the Major was able to dislodge the blockade from the door.

Henry didn't want to let just anyone in and allowed only those who "represented themselves as surgeons" pass through.[32] The first person was twenty-three-year-old army surgeon, Dr. Charles Leale. Wanting to head back into the box, Henry found a Colonel Crawford in the crowd and asked him to stand guard and "prevent other persons from entering the box."[33] Upon his return he found Dr. Leale examining the President.

Dr. Leale arrived for the show earlier in the night and "procured a seat in the dress circle about forty feet from the President's box."[33] In a report written by Leale only hours after Lincoln's death, he stated that when he "entered the box the ladies were very much excited. Mr. Lincoln was seated in a high backed arm-chair with his head leaning towards his right side supported by Mrs. Lincoln who was weeping bitterly. Miss Harris was near her left and behind the President." Leale was still the only doctor on site, and he started to inspect the scene and evaluate the President. The initial discovery of Lincoln found that he was "in a state of general paralysis, his eyes were closed and he was in a profoundly comatose condition, while his breathing was intermittent and exceedingly strenuous."

At this point Rathbone allowed a few more men to enter the box, and Leale "requested them to assist" in placing President Lincoln "in a recumbent position." As they did so Dr. Leale "held his head and shoulders" while his fingers "passed over a large firm clot of blood" at the back of Lincoln's head. Leale "easily removed" the blood clot and "passed the little finger" of his left hand "through the perfectly smooth opening made by the ball." Prior to finding the bullet hole, Leale assumed the President was stabbed, based on Henry's wound. The President wasn't bleeding much and his pulse was barely noticeable. But as soon as Dr. Leale removed his finger from the bullet hole, "a slight oozing of blood followed" and Lincoln's "breathing became more regular."

Leale was soon joined by two other doctors in the Presidential box, Dr. Charles S. Taft and Dr. Albert F. A. King. Leale reported his findings to the other doctors, and they quickly decided that Lincoln must be moved from the Presidential box and to the "nearest house." The idea of taking him to the White House was discussed, but quickly rejected as they assumed the President might die before arriving. Four nearby soldiers were asked to carry Lincoln out of the box, with Leale supporting Lincoln's head. In unison the men lifted Lincoln off the ground, and he was carried on his back out of the Presidential box.

As the men in front carried Lincoln through the dress circle and down the stairs, Henry, Clara, and Mary Todd followed closely behind. When Henry reached the top of the staircase that led to the lobby, he found Major Potter, an army paymaster. Henry's pain was still intense, and with only one good arm, he was of little aid to anyone. So Henry asked Major Potter to assist Mrs. Lincoln. The small group of doctors and victims exited Ford's Theatre, spilling into the perplexed crowd on Tenth Street. The group had trouble determining where to carry the slain President. It was nearly eleven o'clock at night, the street filled with dark houses, and little light was to be found. The noise of the crowd blanketed the directions relayed by Leale and the doctors, making communication difficult.

The sofa Henry Rathbone sat on during the performance. The sofa is still in the Presidential box at Ford's Theatre.
Source: Jennifer Jarrett Teagle

THE ASSASSINATION OF PRESIDENT LINCOLN.
AT FORD'S THEATRE WASHINGTON D.C. APRIL 14TH 1865.

An illustration of the Lincoln Assassination.
Source: Library of congress

Across the street from Ford's Theatre, at 453 Tenth Street, Henry Safford stood on the stoop of the Peterson Boarding house. Safford was a boarder on the second floor and had been watching the scene on Tenth Street after hearing the commotion of the crowd. Safford realized Leale and the others were looking for a place to take Lincoln and called out to them, "Bring him in here!" Upon reaching the Peterson house, a small room in the back was chosen as what would become Lincoln's final resting place. The group of men laid the President in a bed so small that Lincoln's body had to be turned diagonally.

In the foyer hallway, after following the group into the Petersen house, Henry's blood loss was dire. At some point in the night, Clara took a step to stanch the blood by wrapping a handkerchief around the wound. While her actions may have momentarily saved Henry's life, his condition was worsening. General James R. O'Beirne, provost marshal of D.C., arrived at the Peterson house not long after the President and began assessing the situation. Entering the house, O'Beirne observed Henry "standing in the hall bleeding

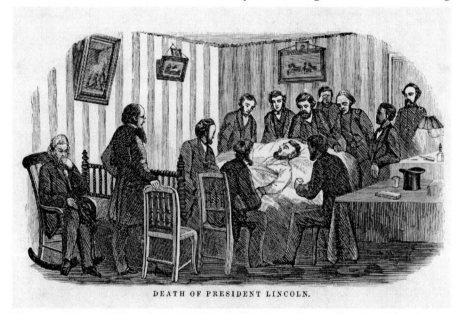

DEATH OF PRESIDENT LINCOLN.

The scene around Lincoln's deathbed at Petersen house. Family, friends and cabinet members stayed by his side the entire night.
Source: Library of Congress

profusely from a wound in the arm, and manifesting some signs of faintness as he slowly moved toward the hall door." The provost marshal exchanged a few words with Henry, and O'Beirne later noted that Henry "did not speak of his own wound" even though it was obvious Rathbone was severely injured. When O'Beirne pointedly asked about Rathbone's arm, Henry responded that it was "only a mere trifle."[34]

Henry's body, however, showed signs that contrasted with his words. Henry was growing increasingly weak from loss of blood and turning pale. Trying to stay engaged in the situation and not distract from the larger concern of Lincoln's well-being, Henry attempted to move toward the sitting room but staggered, finally fainting in the hallway. Henry was not unconscious for long and awoke moments later. O'Beirne felt Henry needed medical attention and helped Henry to his feet. With Clara by his side O'Beirne led Henry down the front steps of the Peterson house and helped place him in a carriage, which quickly took Henry to the home of Senator Harris a few blocks away.[35]

Upon arriving at Senator Harris' home, Henry was helped from the carriage, assisted to a room, and placed on a bed. A call was immediately made for Dr. G.W. Pope to come attend to Henry. Dr. G.W. Pope was an old friend of the Harris family. When Pope entered the Harris home he noticed that "the family and servants were in great excitement and distress." Amidst the calamity, Clara was the only one "who retained sufficient calmness to render assistance and keep order." According to Pope, Clara "was a young lady of remarkable courage and presence of mind in many emergencies." This was a trait that Clara would demonstrate again.

Dr. Pope was taken to Henry's room, where he found the Major "lying on his bed, dress coat, vest, and undergarment being removed, disclosing the wound." Major Rathbone was "as pale as a corpse" and "in a high state of nervous excitement, almost amounting to delirium." The handkerchief that Clara applied earlier in the night had undoubtedly been removed and replaced with sufficient dressing to stop the bleeding. When Dr. Pope was informed of Clara's actions to stanch Henry's bleeding, he pronounced that he greatly doubted "whether any of our modern society women would have been equal to such an emergency, and not have occupied the time in screaming and fainting and hampering the efforts of others."

The doctor continued his investigation and diagnosis of Henry's wound. His notes state that it was "a deep, narrow dagger thrust, clean through the inner part of the left upper arm, close to the armpit, penetrating the biceps muscle and grazing the bone. It came within about one-third of an inch of what is called, in surgical language, the brachial artery and deep basilica vein." It seems that while Henry valiantly attended to the President's situation, he was himself close to the death. According to Pope, "had the blade of the dagger severed those vessels" Rathbone would have "bled to death in about five minutes."

Henry was awake during the doctor's entire examination, and the extreme amount of blood loss put him into an incoherent state. He would frequently shout, "The president is shot – assassinated! He will die! God in Heaven save him! What will become of our country! O, poor, poor, dear Lincoln, our beloved president!"

Dr. Pope continued to dress the wound as Henry wailed about the President. Clara stood by the doctor's side, assisting with "the water, bandages, towels, etc." An army surgeon that had been summoned to the house assisted the doctor in sewing up the wound, which once properly cleansed and bandaged, allowed Henry to finally begin recuperating. The major concern of Henry's wound had been dealt with and brought the family some comfort. Henry too was finally afforded some comfort and fell asleep for the remainder of the night.

A few blocks away at the Peterson house, Lincoln's life slowly drifted away. Surrounded by the men that alternately confided in and confounded the President, they now all sat silently with heavy hearts. Mary Todd and Robert Lincoln were nearby as well, although Mary's uncontrollable nature and outbursts caused her to be sent from the room. In the drawing room, Secretary Stanton was already deep into the investigation of the assassin, questioning witnesses, obtaining evidence and building a case in the unfolding conspiracy.

ALTERNATE THEORY

The details just relayed entail the typically accepted collection of facts regarding the Lincoln assassination. But reports surrounding the Lincoln assassination are rife with inconsistencies and conflicting information. Which might be one reason the assassination still commands so much attention nearly one hundred fifty years later. Because so many bits of information aren't fully conceptualized and so many eyewitness accounts contradict each other, it invites further questioning.

The truth of what really happened that night has been analyzed by every generation. Periodically new facts and theories turn up, trying to decipher the complexity of every likely scenario. The number of questions never seems to dwindle. Why did John Parker leave his post? What would have happened if General Grant had been there? Who drilled the hole in door 7? Were any employees of Ford's Theatre actually a part of the conspiracy? The list goes on and on.

Of course when it comes to Henry Rathbone there are two vital questions. Why didn't he notice John Wilkes Booth enter the state box? And what would have happened if he did?

According to Rathbone, door 8 was open. And judging from Rathbone's location inside the Presidential box, he couldn't see the play very well. The Lincoln Assassination Conspiracy trial transcript of witness James P. Ferguson states that Henry "sat back almost in the corner of the box." This means it's entirely possible that Henry was not watching *Our American Cousin* at all. And sitting directly opposite Booth's entry door increases the likelihood that Henry Rathbone actually encountered Booth prior to the trigger being pulled.

Putting this scenario into the context of Henry's struggle with post-traumatic stress later in life, it would further explain the trauma that Henry dealt with. Although the conventionally accepted version of the details of that night provide enough evidence for symptoms of post-traumatic stress disorder, an even larger failure could have consequences exponentially more severe.

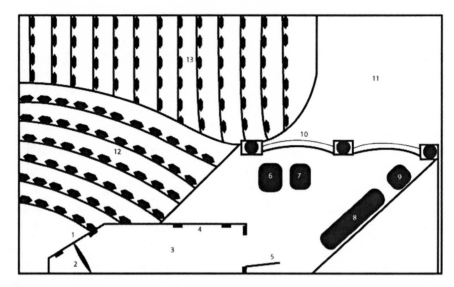

The Assassination Diagram
1. Booth's Entry 2. The bar blocking the entry door 3. The vestibule
4. Door 7 5. Door 8 6. Abraham Lincoln 7. Mary Todd Lincoln
8. Henry Rathbone 9. Clara Harris 10. Railing Booth leapt over 11. The Stage
12. Dress Circle 13. Orchestra level seats

It can be seen from the illustrations and descriptions of the Presidential box that Rathbone had a direct line of sight to John Wilkes Booth entering that night, were Henry to turn even slightly in that direction. Lincoln sat just to the right and slightly forward of door 8. Rathbone sat in line with this door. Through either turning his head or his peripheral vision, Henry had a high probability of seeing someone enter the Presidential box.

Looking at it from the other angle, the first person John Wilkes Booth would have seen was Rathbone. He could have seen him even from the main door. If door 8 was open, then Henry actually may have noticed light from the dress circle as soon as Booth opened the main door. Assuming he didn't see Booth at that point, Booth still would have seen Henry and realized that avoiding Rathbone's attention was, at that moment, the most vital step in reaching his goal.

Just before the shot rang out, Rathbone was approximately seven feet from Booth. Booth's saving grace was the darkness of the hallway. It was the only thing that would have allowed him to enter the box without Henry noticing. Hiding in the shadows and waiting for the time to be right, Booth took refuge in the dark. Clara Harris was well aware of this fact and in afterthought in a letter to a friend she remarked that when thinking "of that fiend barring himself in alone with us, my blood runs cold." But did Booth have to hide in the shadows at all? Maybe Rathbone did notice Booth enter, as the situation seems to dictate. If so, why didn't he stop Booth?

In an article published in the May 5, 1865, edition of *The Public Ledger*, the details of the scenario lend themselves to the argument that Rathbone noticed Booth before the shot. The article, printed only twenty days after the assassination, shares the exact same details as the normally accepted facts up until the moment when John Wilkes Booth enters the State box. After Booth enters, however, the article states that Rathbone met the assassin at the door to box 8.

According to *The Public Ledger*, Clara Harris stated that Booth actually entered the box earlier in the night, before finally returning at 10:13 to shoot Lincoln. In her statement, Clara noted that "nearly one hour before the commission of the deed the assassin came to the door of the box, and, looked in to take survey of the position of its occupants." At this time it was thought that Booth's appearance was either "a mistake or the exercise of impertinent curiosity." Clara continued to recount that when Booth came back to kill Lincoln, "Major Rathbone arose and asked the intruder his business. He rushed past the Major without making a reply, and placing his pistol close to the back of the President's head actually in contact with it, fired."[36] These same words are also referenced in Jim Bishop's 1955 book, *The Day Lincoln Was Shot*. According to Bishop, this account of Clara's was given to Secretary of War Edwin Stanton, during Stanton's interrogation of witnesses from a room inside the Peterson house.

This story of the events seems equally as plausible as the one we're accustomed to hearing. Rathbone, being seated behind the rest of the party, most likely would have seen Booth walk through the open doorway. Rising to meet the killer at the door, the quick actions of Booth would have caught Rathbone by surprise, not giving Henry a chance to react properly, especially considering the close proximity Booth had to Lincoln. Henry most likely would not have expected an attack and so would not have been on guard. It would have been a mistake that, later in life, may have ground away in Henry's mind.

A note to add to both of these accounts is that theatergoers that night mentioned that just before the shot rang out, Lincoln stared blankly into the audience. His head turned slightly to the left and his eyes gazed in no particular direction. Was this Lincoln's way of attending to the sounds of Rathbone confronting Booth directly behind him?

So which account is true? Most historians fall on the side of the original tale and see Rathbone getting caught up in the play. However, when you consider Rathbone sitting in a dark theater, with a bad view of the show, late at night, the possibility of him being more interested in a man entering the box starts to gain credence. Allowing Booth to enter and rush past him would further explain his complete breakdown later in life. Not only did he let the assailant go free, but he had the opportunity to prevent the entire event from ever taking place. If for no other reason than public embarrassment and utter disdain, Rathbone may have hidden the fact that he let Booth pass him. He couldn't let the public know that he actually encountered Booth before the fatal shot was fired.

In Clara's official affidavit of that night's events her story is changed from what she allegedly relayed to Secretary Stanton. The story she gave Stanton was fresh in her mind, only hours after the assassination. Her official affidavit was given a few days later after having time to compare notes with Henry. In fact, Clara gave her own affidavit of the events following Henry's, and in this affidavit it declares that she "read the foregoing affidavit of Major Rathbone, and knows the contents thereof." This means she was able to match her story exactly to whatever Henry said. In order to protect her step-brother and fiancé, Clara was given every opportunity to ensure her story conformed to Henry's. They both stated they were "intently observing the proceedings upon the stage," and Henry made a point of saying his back was "towards the door," possibly as a way to ensure their story was not questioned.

Unfortunately the precise details of what happened inside the Presidential box during those moments can never be completely known. Other events that night with several eyewitness accounts are still being argued, so with only two accounts of the actual attack, there is even less to work with. This fact however has its advantages and disadvantages as many times more opinions and eyewitness accounts don't mean the information will be clearer.

One final aspect to note when reviewing the first-hand accounts of Henry, Clara and the plethora of other individuals is the validity of eyewitness testimony. In 1865, there were few other types of evidence for investigators to pursue. There was no security footage to comb through or DNA samples to collect. They only had eyewitness testimony to base their investigation on. Filtering through rumors and hearsay, the prosecutors and defense teams had to delineate what was truth and what was fiction. This is a difficult task regardless of the time period.

As forensic science improved over the years, the value of eyewitness testimony dwindled considerably. According to the Innocence Project, an organization "dedicated to exonerating wrongfully convicted people through DNA testing", "eyewitness misidentification is the single greatest cause of wrongful convictions" in the United States. This is partly due to the fallibility of the human mind. Memories are subjective and open to external influence, causing moments to alter in the mind. This is especially true for a witness that deals with tragedy or when their memories are deeply affected by emotions. This results in memories that differ from the truth of what actually happened. These differences can range from small insignificant details to major elements of an account. In the account of Henry's interaction with John Wilkes Booth, the difference is whether Henry confronted the assassin before or after the shooting.

6
A World Without Lincoln

At 7:22 a.m. on the morning after the shooting, Abraham Lincoln was pronounced dead. Rain poured from the clouds hovering over Washington D.C., deepening the somber mood of the nation's capital. The news of Lincoln's death spread quickly through the city. As the day progressed, the rest of the United States received the information through telegraph wires, newspapers, and word of mouth. In the South, the news traveled a bit slower. Confederate President Jefferson Davis received the news four days later on April 19. His response was ambivalent at best, saying: "If it were to be done, it were better it were well done."[1]

Within days, the entire country was abuzz with the news, and although the majority was morose, there were also reports of celebration. Henry received the news in bed. Whether he was awoken to receive the news or if he was allowed to rest and get the information later in the day is not known. The gash in his arm received from John Wilkes Booth was still fresh, and the horrific trauma was still only hours old.

Henry spent most of the next few days in terrible pain. His left arm was kept immobilized, and he wouldn't regain use of it for several months; by some accounts his arm was never the same again.[2] The physician, G.W. Pope, visited the house daily, and in a short time Henry recovered his strength and calmness of mind.[3] The moments of that night would be with him forever, though, and with the event so fresh in his mind it is likely they overshadowed all other thoughts he had.

Imaginably, as he lay recuperating in bed, each time he closed his eyes to rest, flashbacks of that night played through his mind. His dreams would have been haunting, but lying awake in bed, his arm throbbing in pain, would have brought little relief from the events of that fateful night. Every aspect probably replayed in his mind, creating an internal cacophony of screams, gunshots, laughter, and sobbing. The attack, the blood, the hysteria, and the horror of the entire night would have been relentless. There was no way for Henry to escape his mind's eye.

As Henry rested and healed, Clara became involved in the investigation. As she proved by her actions in attempting to save Henry's life, Clara was strong willed and quick thinking. The events surrounding the assassination undoubtedly weighed heavily on her mind as well. Clara was not one to shy away, however, and her thirst for answers was much stronger than any trepidation she had of reliving that night's events. Upon learning that a few investigators would be inspecting the scene of the crime, Clara requested to join them.

Her recollections would provide insight to the men accompanying her, and Clara had some lingering questions of her own. The assassination and the moments that followed had transpired so quickly. For Clara, revisiting the scene might have provided closure. Something that Henry was not afforded.

On Sunday morning, April 16, the day after Lincoln's death, Clara accompanied a group of men to Ford's Theatre. Among them was Clara's father, Ira Harris, Supreme Court Judge A.B. Olin, Judge Carter, and James P. Ferguson, owner of the saloon connected to Ford's Theatre. Their intention was to inspect the Presidential box and the scene of the crime. With candles in hand the investigators made their way into the box and first inspected the hole in door 7.[4] It was suspected at the time that Booth actually shot through the door and not at point blank range. After some

Abraham Lincoln Funeral Procession through the streets of Washington.
Source: Library of Congress

quick detective work, it was verified this was not the case as it was clear the hole had been carved out with a knife or gimlet.

Clara had other things on her mind. James Ferguson remembered her remarking, "There is one thing I want to examine. I am satisfied there was a bar across the door when I jumped off my seat and called for assistance." This remark makes one wonder if Clara played a larger role inside the Presidential box than is commonly notated. It's probable that Clara herself attempted to open the door as Henry recovered slowly. However, finding the hold of the bar too strong, it required the little strength Henry had left to jar it loose.

The group that morning further inspected the door and the wall opposite it. There they found a "square hole cut in the wall, just big enough to let in a bar."[5]

The party confirmed that the hole was directly across from the door and it looked as though it had been cut with a penknife. After a short while Clara and the men left the theater. As Clara

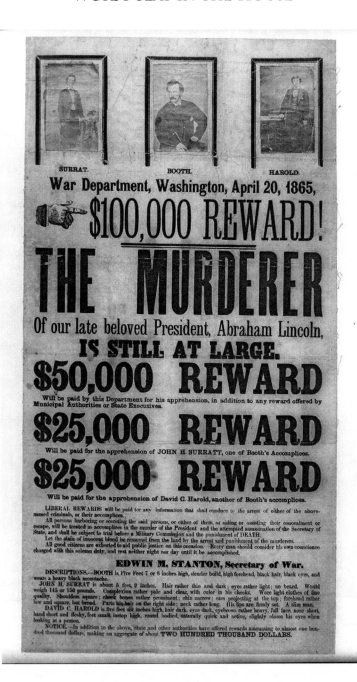

Reward Poster for the remaining conspirators in the Lincoln Assassination. From left to right, John Surratt, John Wilkes Booth, and David Harold. Source: Library of Congress

left she was required to walk the same path she had taken only two days prior, undoubtedly providing a surreal recollection of the events of that horrifying night.

The next day, Monday, April 17, Clara met with Judge Olin once again. This time, however, it was to give her sworn affidavit of the assassination events. Henry, too, gave his sworn affidavit at this time. Whether Judge Olin came to the Harris home to obtain the affidavits is not clear, but it is quite possible as Henry was still recovering from his wound. As mentioned previously, Henry gave his affidavit first, followed by Clara. Her details matched Henry's exactly, putting them at odds with what she allegedly told Secretary Stanton three days earlier at the Petersen house.

The nation's capital was in a near frenzy. John Wilkes Booth was still on the run, and every home in Washington was being searched. The investigators, under the watchful eye of Secretary Stanton, made arrests almost daily and quickly brought in the

The conspirators David Herold, Lewis Powell, George Atzerodt, and Mary Surratt were found guilty in conspiracy and sentenced to death. This is moments before their hanging in the courtyard of the Old Arsenal Building in D.C., July 7, 1865. Source: Library of Congress

band of conspirators involved in the assassination. Stanton was allowed to retain his position throughout the investigation and trial, as incoming President Andrew Johnson declared that the conspirators would be tried by a military commission.

As the hunt for John Wilkes Booth continued, Lincoln's body was prepared for viewing and burial. The funeral was held on Monday, April 19, in the East Room of the White House. In the book *Washington in Lincoln's Time*, written by reporter and Lincoln friend Noah Brooks, a list of all notable attendees is given. Henry and Clara are not mentioned among them. Mary Todd Lincoln and son Tad were also not present, as they were sealed up in the Lincolns' bedroom. Mary didn't leave the White House for nearly five weeks.

Henry's absence was excusable as his wounds were still relatively fresh. Secretary Seward and his son Frederick also didn't attend, still recuperating from the attack by Lewis Powell.

After the assassination, Ford's Theatre was guarded by the military during the conspiracy trial. Congress purchased the building, turning it into an office building. Today Ford's Theatre is a museum and a place of live theater for the public.
Source: Library of Congress

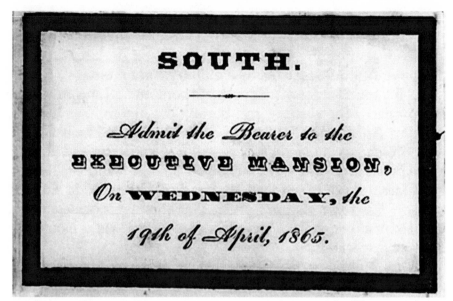

A pass to the funeral of Abraham Lincoln held at the White House on
April 19, 1865.
Source: Library of Congress

Clara undoubtedly felt the need to stay with Henry and be by
his side. With Mary Todd Lincoln not attending, although Clara
would want to pay her respects to the President, she was not
needed to support her dear friend.

The White House funeral was the first of many viewings of the
body of Abraham Lincoln. The President's remains and those of
his young son, Willie Lincoln, who died three years earlier, were
being taken back to Illinois by train. The funeral train was to retrace
the same route Lincoln followed on his inaugural train. It made
thirteen stops along way, stopping in six states to allow the citizens
of the nation to join the mourning process.

Around 11:00 p.m. on the night of April 25, the funeral train
arrived in east Albany, New York. His body was shipped across
the Hudson River and moved into the capitol building for the
thousands who had lined up to see their slain leader one last
time. On April 26 the doors to the viewing room in the capitol
were opened at 1:15 a.m. and did not close until 1:30 p.m. Henry
and Clara were not there, although they intended to travel back
to Albany as soon as possible.

On the same day Lincoln's body arrived in Albany, Clara penned a letter to a friend detailing her thoughts on the recent events of her life.

Washington April 25th

My Dear Mary:

I received your kind note last week, & should have answered it before, but that I have really felt, as though (I) could not settle myself quietly, even to the performance of such a slight duty as that. Henry has been suffering a great deal with his arm, but it is now doing very well. The knife went from the elbow nearly to the shoulder, inside, cutting an artery, nerves & veins. He bled so profusely as to make him very weak. My whole clothing, as I sat in the box, was saturated liberally with blood, & my hands & face – you may imagine what a scene – poor Mrs. Lincoln all through that dreadful night would look at me with horror & scream, "oh! My husband's blood, my dear husband's blood" – which it was not, though I did not know it at the time. The President's wound did not bleed externally at all. The brain was instantly suffused.

When I sat down to write, I did not intend alluding to these fearful events at all, but I really cannot fix my mind on anything else – though I try my best to think of them as little as possible. I cannot sleep, & really feel wretchedly – only to think that fiend is still at large. There was a report here yesterday that every house in the District of Columbia was to be searched to-day. I hoped it was true, as the impression seems to be gaining ground that Booth is hidden in Washington. Is not that a terrible thought!

Mr. Johnson (former Vice President Andrew Johnson) is at present living in Mr. Hooper's house opposite us – a guard are walking the street in front constantly.

It will probably be two or three weeks before Mrs. Lincoln will be able to make arrangements for leaving. She has not left her bed since she returned to the White House that morning.

We expect to be able to leave next week for New York, but on what day, it would be impossible yet to say. I will write you in time however, so that I shall be sure to see you while there.

Please give my love to all the family, & believe me.

Very truly yours,
Clara H.

(Courtesy of The New-York Historical Society. American Historical Manuscripts Collection - Harris, Clara)

In examining Clara's letter we find it contains multiple interesting points. At the time of the letter, Clara states that Henry was doing "very well." It's unclear how subjective those words are and whether they refer to his physical state relative to the drastic state he was in on assassination night, but he seemed to have improved a great deal. One of the more enlightening points that Clara makes is that the blood she was covered in was not Abraham Lincoln's blood. There has been much discussion about how much the President actually bled. According to Dr. Leale's report and Clara, Lincoln's wound only bled sporadically, many times only when Leale removed a freshly formed blood clot.

Henry's wound we know bled profusely, and many times his blood was mistaken for the President's, on items such as the bar blocking the main door to the Presidential box and possibly actress Laura Keene's dress. After the fact, Clara was aware it was Henry's blood and informs her reader in graphic detail. The image of Clara wandering along Tenth Street, saturated with blood as she made her way to the Peterson house, allows us to more closely empathize with her.

Clara also remarks on how hard it is for her to "fix" her mind on anything other than the assassination. She finds it difficult to sleep and makes note of the guards constantly on patrol in front of President Andrew Johnson's temporary residence. He was living in Congressman Samuel Hooper's home on H Street, while Mary Todd Lincoln mourned at the White House, preventing Johnson from moving in.

The apprehension of Booth, it seemed, would provide Clara some needed closure. Knowing that the assassin was still at large seemed to haunt Clara. She was afraid of the unknown and desired the respite of Booth's capture to still her nerves. Fortunately her wish was granted the next day. On April 26, twelve days after pulling the trigger, John Wilkes Booth was shot and killed at Garrett's farm, near Port Royal, Virginia.

With Lincoln's body gone from the city and John Wilkes Booth dead, the proximity of the assassination was diminishing. Time was beginning to heal the emotional wounds little by little, and Henry was recovering. The couple still intended to make the trip back to Albany, where Henry could fully recuperate in the comfort of his hometown, surrounded by friends and family. Set to begin on May 1, the conspiracy trial for Lincoln's assassination was fast approaching, however, and Henry would be required to testify.

Clara filled the time writing friends and informing them of Henry and her wellbeing. One such letter was printed in an 1889 edition of *The Washington Post*, in an article stating the letter was originally printed by Andrew James Symington in *The Independent*. In this article the letter, dated four days after the first letter, was written by Clara Harris to a friend referred to only as "M." Once again Clara reminisces about the assassination night events.

Washington, April 29

My Dear M,

I was very glad to hear from you again, your letter proving that in all the events of your matronly life our old friendship is not forgotten. You may well say that we have been passing through scenes sad indeed. That terrible Friday night is to me yet almost like some dreadful vision. I have been very intimate with Mrs. Lincoln and the family ever since our mutual residence in Washington, which began at the same time, and we have been constantly in the habit of driving and going to the opera and theater together. It was the only amusement, with the exception of receiving at their own house, in which the President and Mrs. Lincoln were permitted, according to custom, to indulge, and to escape from the crowds who constantly thronged to see them, more than from any decided taste for such things. They were in the habit of going very often to hear Forrest, Booth, Hackett, and such actors when playing in Washington.

The night before the murder was that of the general illumination here, and they drove all through the streets to see it; a less calculating villain might have taken that opportunity for his crime, or the night before, when the White House alone was brilliantly illuminated and the figure of the President stood out in full relief to the immense crowd below, who stood in the darkness to listen to his speech. He spoke from the center window of the Executive Mansion. I had been invited to pass the evening there, and stood at the window of an adjoining room with Mrs. Lincoln watching the crowd below as they listened and cheered. Of course, Booth was there, watching his chance. I wonder that he did not choose that occasion, but probably he knew a better opportunity would be offered. After the speech was over we went into Mr. Lincoln's room; he was lying on the sofa, quite exhausted; but he talked of the events of the past fortnight, of his visit to Richmond, of the enthusiasm everywhere felt through the country; and Mrs. Lincoln declared the past few days to have been the happiest of her life. Their prospects indeed seemed fair — peace dawning upon our land and four years of a happy and honored rule before one of the gentlest, best, and loveliest men I ever knew. I never saw him out of temper- the kindest husband, the tenderest father, the truest friend, as well as the wisest statesman. "Our Beloved President" — when I think that I shall never again stand in his genial presence, that I have lost his friendship so tried and true, I feel like putting on the robe of mourning which the country wears.

My own dear father was deeply attached to Mr. Lincoln; they thoroughly sympathized in many things, and Mr. Lincoln, perhaps, being able to discern in him an honest, unselfish nature, in that akin to his own, was wont with him to throw off the restraints of the politician and talk over things as with an old friend. The shock has been a terrible one to him; he feels his death to be a deep personal affliction. You are right in supposing the Major Rathbone who was with us to be the "Henry" you knew in Albany.

We four composed the party that evening. They drove to our door in the gayest spirits, chatting on the way — and the President was received with the greatest enthusiasm. They say we were watched by the assassins; aye, as we alighted from the carriage. Oh, how could any one be so cruel as to strike that dear, kind, honest face? And when I think of the fiend barring himself in alone with us, my blood runs cold. My dress is saturated with blood; my hands and face were covered. You may imagine what a scene, and so, all through that dreadful night when we stood by that dying bed. Poor Mrs. Lincoln was and is almost crazy.

Henry narrowly escaped with his life. The knife was struck at his heart with all the force of a practiced and powerful arm; he fortunately parried the blow, and received a wound in his arm, extending along the bone from the elbow nearly to the shoulder. He concealed it for some time, but was finally carried home in a swoon; the loss of blood had been so great from an artery and veins severed. He is now getting quite well, but cannot yet use his arm.

I hope you will pardon me this dreadfully long letter. I have been quite ill, and have as yet answered scarcely any of the numerous letters I have received in the last two weeks.

Ever yours sincerely,
Clara H. Harris

Similar to the previous letter, this letter is chock full of details of and insight into the life of Henry and Clara. She commented on her close relationship with Mary Todd Lincoln and how the two became close friends after having arrived in Washington under similar circumstances. Mary was comfortable with Clara and the entire Harris family. She seemed to enjoy the company of the young girl and delighted in spending evenings out with her. It was during one of these outings that Clara discussed her attendance at the White House a few nights before the assassination, watching as President Lincoln addressed a group of listeners from a window.

Clara mentions Booth twice in this letter. Once in reference to the speech from the window and again when discussing the assassination. Despite the fact that John Wilkes Booth had been caught three days earlier, thoughts of the killer still haunted her. In this letter, Clara is fixated on the idea that Booth had watched the party before committing his act. The thought of Booth watching from the street and then waiting in the shadows to make his move made "her blood run cold." The idea that the killer may have been watching them dominated her thoughts. To Clara, the fact that Booth was in effect stalking them, added to the macabre aftereffects of the event.

The close of Clara's letter discussed the wellbeing of Henry. His physical standing seemed to be improving, but his arm was not yet usable. There's no record of his mental state at this point, but so soon after the assassination it can be assumed the entire city was a bit overwhelmed.

A little more than a week after this letter was written, on May 9, 1865, the Military Commission for the trial of the assassination conspirators convened for the first time. The trial was held at the Old Arsenal Building in Washington, and the testimony of witnesses was scheduled to begin a few days later on May 12. Henry provided his sworn testimony on May 15, 1865, exactly one month after the death of Abraham Lincoln.

His testimony at the trial was almost exactly the same, word for word, as the sworn testimony he gave Judge Olin on April 17. One item of note was that Henry stated the time that elapsed between the discharge of the pistol and when John Wilkes Booth leapt from the Presidential box didn't exceed thirty seconds. This helps paint a more vivid picture of the action that took place in those mere moments.

In court, Rathbone is also presented a Bowie knife with a seven-inch blade, which is still caked with bloodstains. When Henry was questioned if the knife was indeed the one that Booth wielded that evening, Henry is unsure. He stated the "knife might have made a wound similar to the one I received. The assassin held the blade in a horizontal position, I think, and the nature of the wound would indicate it; it came down with a sweeping blow from above." But he could not positively identify it as the same knife. The knife nevertheless was offered in evidence.

The trial continued for another six weeks after Henry's testimony, and on June 30, 1865, the final verdicts and sentences were determined. David Herold, Lewis Powell, George

President Abraham Lincoln's railroad funeral car.
Source: Library of Congress

The Lincoln Assassination Conspirators: In the middle, John Wilkes Booth.
Starting at the top, moving clockwise is George Atzerodt, Edman Spangler,
Michael O'Laughlin, Lewis Powell, Samuel Arnold, and David Herold.
Source: Library of Congress

Henry Rathbone, sometime after the assassination, date not known.
Source: Rathbone Family Historian

Atzerodt, and Mary Surratt were sentenced to death, making Surratt the first woman executed by the United States federal government. Three other conspirators, Michael O'Laughlen, Samuel Arnold, and Dr. Samuel Mudd, were sentenced to life in prison. Edmund Spangler was sentenced to six years in prison. The four sentenced to death were brought to the courtyard of the Old Arsenal Building on July 7, 1865, and led to the gallows built specifically for this day. At 1:30 p.m. the order was given and all were executed by hanging.

Henry and Clara finally went back to Albany, where Henry continued his recovery. According to friends, Henry spent six weeks or more at the home of his cousin, Julia Rathbone. The family spared no expense in the treatment of his arm, and Henry was provided the best surgeons and doctors in Albany. Despite these measures Henry's arm was never the same, losing full strength in it as the years passed on.[6]

While Henry recovered with the help of his cousin and other family members, Clara undoubtedly enjoyed her time away from Washington D.C. It was a chance to clear her thoughts and be away from the scene of the crime. Although the relatives there possibly barraged her with questions about the assassination, she wasn't involved in the trial or reminded of Abraham and Mary Todd whenever she passed by the White House. In Albany she was surrounded by childhood memories and welcoming images that put her at ease.

The couple couldn't stay long in Albany as Henry had to return to his job at the disbursing branch of the Provost Marshal General's Bureau. His work there at first probably provided Henry a reprieve from the daily thoughts that besieged his mind. The habits, procedure, and paperwork provided a welcome structure to his thoughts. This distraction however was probably only temporary and waned over time.

In August 1866 he transferred to the recruitment and organizing account division within the disbursing office, but the office life may have been wearing thin on him. Henry and Clara's wedding had officially been scheduled for July, and they intended for the wedding to be held in Albany. In March 1867 the term for Senator

Ira Harris was ending and he intended to move back to Albany, where he would take a position as professor at the Albany Law School. So the soon-to-be-married couple would need their own place to live in Washington. With everything else changing and their plans for the future still up in the air, Henry must have felt it was a good time to change positions.

Just before Henry left for Albany, he was required to testify in one more trial. The trial of John Surratt was being held before a district court in Washington D.C. The trial was in June of 1867, and Henry obliged the request to testify. He offered his stock version of events, nothing varied from the story he'd given eighteen months earlier.[7] After the trial had concluded, Henry seemed ready to move on. He left Washington D.C., resigned his volunteer commission, and took a leave of absence from the army. The recorded reason for the absence was "to visit Europe."[8]

7

Marriage and Family

Henry and Clara's engagement seemed to last longer than expected. With the announcement coming before the assassination, maybe the couple wanted to allow the tragedy to completely pass so they could fully tend to any residual emotional wounds. But after the long wait, the ceremony was finally held on July 11, 1867. Held at the Emmanuel Baptist Church in Albany, the ceremony was performed by the new reverend of the church, Dr. Charles DeWitt Bridgman.[1] After the wedding, Senator Harris held a reception at his house, and "among the distinguished guests in attendance was Chief Justice Chase."[2]

After the wedding the couple stayed around Albany for the summer. They visited their family in the summer home of Ira Harris in Loudonville, NY. It wasn't far from the Albany home on Eagle Street, where Henry and Clara stayed most of the trip.[3] How odd it must have been for Henry to return to his boyhood home and reflect on all that life had served up to that point? The house may have stirred up memories of his father, which mixed with those of Lincoln. He was on the verge of a new direction in his life. His military career was on hold, and he was married to the woman he loved. The same woman that held true to him after that assassin's blade had been thrust into his arm. She was the woman Henry needed then and the one he wanted to keep forever.

After their summer stay in Albany, the newlyweds were off to Europe. It's not certain how long the couple was overseas or where their destinations. Henry obtained a passport the same month of his wedding, however, and with his leave of absence filed as a request to visit Europe, it can be assumed it was not a short trip.

Upon returning to the United States the couple decided to make their home in Washington, D.C. In an interesting decision,

Rev. Dr. Charles DeWitt Bridgman, Emmanuel Baptist Church.

the couple purchased the house at 706 Jackson Place.[4] It was a lovely and expensive house in affluent and politically centered Lafayette Square. In fact, the house was located directly across the street from the White House. It's not certain why Henry chose this house. It seems to go against reason for a man coping with failure to protect a President slain in his presence. Maybe it was a way for Henry to honor Abraham Lincoln. It's possible that Henry didn't want to forget. He may even have harbored a subconscious need to constantly face the fear and regret.

The young couple lived alone for the first few years of their marriage. Henry was still in the regular army and was involved in some aspects. On December 3, 1867, he was brevetted lieutenant-colonel for his services connected with the organization of the Volunteer armies. Henry also showed up for military events, such as in 1869 when he was a part of President Ulysses S. Grant's inaugural procession. Henry was a deputy marshal along the route and was charged with organizing the

712 Jackson Place, Washington D.C. This is the first home Henry and Clara purchased together after getting married. At the time it was 706 Jackson Place. The home is in the affluent Lafayette Square directly across from the White House.

This is the view of the White House from the front steps of 712 Jackson Place.

officers of the Army, Navy, and Marine Corps not attached to other organizations.[5]

In 1870, the couple welcomed their first child into the family. And in a very odd coincidence, Henry Riggs Rathbone was born on February 12, Abraham Lincoln's would-be 61st birthday. With the five-year anniversary of Lincoln's assassination only two months away, this was sure to rustle emotions and memories in both Clara and Henry. Every year the boy's birthday would serve as a reminder of that night. To Henry, the coincidence of having his oldest son linked forever to Lincoln had to be bittersweet.

Also in 1870, Henry officially resigned his commission in the regular Army. From that point on he never again had any regular occupation.[6] He was able to live off the large fortune that he inherited from his father, as well as the money he had earned himself over the past decade. According to the 1870 Washington D.C. census, he reported a value of fifty thousand dollars in real estate and fifty thousand dollars in personal worth.

In his early retirement Henry was able to stay busy by continuing his involvement in Washington D.C. politics and society functions, undoubtedly abetted by living directly across from the White House. It was reminiscent of what Henry's father had done by purchasing the home on Eagle Street, positioning himself across from the New York State Capitol.

Clara was a remarkable asset to Henry both personally and socially. She was well traveled and highly educated and was remarked to shine in "society as a brilliant conversationalist and fascinating woman."[7] Henry, on the other hand, was different following the assassination, as noted by those who knew him best. His close friends noticed how he brooded over that fateful night at Ford's Theatre. They said he blamed himself for not having been more alert.[8] As much as Henry tried to put on a good show and move on with his life, it seemed that a terrible inner torment would not let go of him.

But Henry wouldn't let the pain and regret prevent him from attempting to live a full life and building a family with Clara. In August 1871, the couple welcomed another son to the family, Gerald Laurence Rathbone. One year later, in September 1872,

Henry Rathbone in 1871.
Source: Rathbone Family Historian

they welcomed their daughter, Clara Pauline Rathbone, into the world. Everything in life seemed promising for Henry and Clara. By 1873, they had three wonderful children, a great house, and since Henry didn't have to work, they had plenty of time together as a family. But unseen by others, Henry's mind was crumbling.

Eight years had passed since the assassination, but the hard-hitting symptoms of Henry's mental illness may have been delayed. The ruminations and physical ailments related to his guilt may have laid dormant, waiting for something to finally push Henry over the edge. It's unsure whether something finally clicked inside Henry or whether his mental illness simply followed a gradual process, but more people began noticing odd behavior in him.

As it turned out, the ease of Henry's life may have been a detriment, rather than a luxury. He had nothing to distract him from endlessly replaying the events of April 14. There was nothing to prevent him from looking out his front window and staring upon the White House, where his mind could drift to the man who once resided behind the walls. Was this his new routine? Did thinking of Lincoln and Booth become a daily habit? Even social events were not much of a distraction. In 1874, there was an article in the *Evening Star*, a Washington newspaper, that listed Mrs. Colonel Rathbone as an attendee of a charity ball for the benefit of the Children's Hospital. Henry wasn't listed among those in attendance.[9]

In December 1875, the Rathbone family received terrible news. Clara's father, Senator Ira Harris, had passed away at the age of seventy-three in his home in Albany. He was buried in the Albany Rural Cemetery with his first and second wives, Clarissa and Louisa. Clara and Henry made the trip to Albany for the funeral services.[10] The same reverend who married the couple, Dr. Charles DeWitt Bridgman, presided over the senator's funeral.

Henry may have visited the burial site of his father while at the cemetery. Jared Lewis Rathbone's gravesite was only a short walk away. At thirty-eight years old, Henry now had lost two fathers. The first was probably more of a memory, but still a legend in his mind. The second was a man who had provided direction, guidance, and most importantly, the woman he loved and married. And around this time, without a father figure to offer inspiration or guidance, Henry's life quickly grew more difficult.

After the funeral of Senator Harris, the Rathbone family started traveling to Europe in winter months and living in Washington during the summer.[11] Although the main reason for their travel was the education of the children,[12] there are signs that Henry's physical stability was diminishing at this time as well. He was suffering from a disease known as dyspepsia, which is a form of chronic indigestion. It causes nausea, heartburn, vomiting, and many times an ulcer. This disease was most likely a direct reflection of his mental stability as dyspepsia has been linked to high anxiety, depression, and post-traumatic stress disorder in veterans.[13] Henry's mind was fooling his body, and now both were under extreme hardship. Traveling to Europe may also have served as an attempt at discovering medicine to help Henry with his ailments.

When Henry and the family returned to Washington in 1877, they had a new neighbor in the White House. Rutherford B. Hayes succeeded Ulysses Grant as President of the United States in March 1877, and Rathbone had hopes for a position with the new administration. Henry had not worked in approximately seven years and may have assumed his presence in Washington and the help of his close friends with political power could help him obtain a position with the new administration. But it didn't. This wasn't due to lack of effort.

According to the National Archives, there are sixty-two pages of letters on file from the time period of 1877 to 1885 recommending Henry for appointment to various consular posts. Many of these letters came from highly esteemed individuals such as General William Sherman, Admiral David Porter, and General Ambrose Burnside. The clout carried by these names seems to have made little impact. In the end, despite numerous inaccurate reports that Henry was the U.S. Consul for Hanover, Germany, he never received any appointment under the Department of State.

A major factor in the decision to deny him an appointment may have been his noticeable defects in personality, manner, and attitude. Henry's mental difficulties were becoming more apparent, and they were manifesting themselves in new ways. Although normally reserved, Henry was known to possess a fiery nature and was growing more prone to violent outbursts.[14] Undoubtedly, many of these outbursts came at the expense of Clara. Over time his quiet demeanor took on the traits of jealousy, nervousness, and suspicion. His fears were irrational, and his actions reflected such senseless thoughts. Henry's jealousy ballooned to the point he would not tolerate any man paying Clara notice. He was also growing weary of the attention that Clara gave to their children. In his mind he deserved to occupy her every thought.

In the fall of 1878, the Rathbone family continued their trend of traveling to Europe in the winter months. Sailing on the S.S. Seythia, Henry, Clara, and the three children made their annual journey overseas to continue the education of Henry Riggs, Gerald, and young Clara.[15] Henry also planned to continue his search for a cure for his mental and physical ailments. He had high hopes for the hot springs of Carlsbad. In the late nineteenth century, Carlsbad, now known as Karlovy Vary in western Bohemia, Czech Republic, was a renowned spa city. Visitors and tourists traveled from all around the world to steep themselves in the hot spring water. Visitors to Carlsbad suffered from all sorts of illness, with dyspepsia being the most common.

According to the 1886 book, *Carlsbad and its Environs*, "at least two-thirds of the patients to be met at Carlsbad go there in order to obtain from the waters relief from the varied forms of indigestion. When the dyspepsia is simple and idiopathic it is generally cured in a complete and easy manner by the use of the Carlsbad waters." The problem for Henry was that his dyspepsia wasn't simple and it wasn't idiopathic, as it most likely was directly correlated to his anxiety and depression. So after seeking out a cure to his problems at Carlsbad, Henry returned from the spring worse off than when he arrived.[16]

The years passed by and the Rathbones continued alternating between Europe and the United States, although in later years they predominantly stayed in Europe. When in the U.S. the family

A panoramic view of the city of Carlsbad, known for it's healing hot springs. Henry visited the springs in a search to find a cure for his dyspepsia. Today Carlsbad is known as Karlovy Vary, in Bohemia, Czech Republic.
Source: *Carlsbad and its Environs*

typically stayed in their Washington D.C. home in Lafayette Square, and on occasion they would visit their relatives in Albany. Before a planned trip to Germany, the Rathbones made one of these trips to Albany prior to catching a steamship in New York City.

The family spent some time at the Harris farm in Loudonville. At the house the family was content at times. When Henry was occupied his mind was not able to wander and he enjoyed the presence of his children. Throughout much of the time in Albany he devoted three hours a day to reading history with his two sons, who may have distracted him just enough, allowing him to focus his thoughts on the present.[17] But this was not the norm, and the strain of Henry's manner was taking a toll on Clara.

While in Albany, the possibility of separating and leaving Henry was discussed. Clara was reluctant to give up on Henry and she could not bear to be apart from her children. It was also felt that while Henry's depression and anger were a concern, his regular "manner with his wife and children was so affectionate, his disposition so gentle, that they felt that he was better with them than he would be in the custody of strangers."[18] Henry's paranoia and anxiety was now ever present. He always traveled armed and prided himself on his superior marksmanship.[19] He even had a need to express this fact to those around him, making it known that he could handle any situation that required the use of a gun and that he was a sure shot. This was just one sign that the assassination was still on his mind seventeen years later.

According to an Albany friend, Henry was demented later in life due to the worry that he had disappointed the nation by not protecting the President. Rathbone stressed that the public had expected him to prevent John Wilkes Booth from killing Lincoln. Despite assurance of friends this wasn't the case, Rathbone never believed them. Henry was so overcome with thoughts of the assassination he could rarely stay on point. During conversations he consistently veered from the subject and brought up the topic of Lincoln's death.[20]

During this time, in 1882, it wasn't just Henry's mental state that was degenerating, but his physical state as well. His dyspepsia seemed to grow worse every year. His uncle, Hamilton

Harris, noted this fact when Henry stopped by Harris' law office one day in Albany. Henry's physical appearance was so poor that Hamilton asked him what was wrong. Henry responded with such vivid details of his excruciating dyspepsia that it left an indelible impression on Harris.

When it was time to depart for Germany, the Harris family still had some apprehension regarding the safety of Clara and the children. Clara herself was unsure, and requested that her sister Louise accompany them as the children's nanny.[21] Louise obliged and joined the family on their trip to Hanover, Germany. Otherwise, Clara may not have accompanied Henry.

The family seemed to enjoy their time in Hanover and spent the summer and fall of 1883 in a large apartment in town. They planned to stay in Hanover throughout the winter as well. Christmas was quickly approaching, and the family enjoyed filling the chilly December days with shopping and holiday fun. But Henry's disposition did not match that of the season. Over the past few months he'd grown "very irritable and developed hallucinations that gave his wife great alarm." The most persistent of these hallucinations was that Clara "was planning to leave him and take the children away. He continually begged her with great earnestness not to do so, but no assurance seemed to satisfy him."[22]

8
LIVING WITH A "SOLDIER'S HEART"

The evolution of our understanding of mental illness has a twisting and confusing history. A prime example can be found in the study of post-traumatic stress disorder (PTSD). Following the trail of PTSD, one can see how improvements in science and medicine alter the understanding of this mental illness. With each new study more information is learned and folded into what was known before. Sometimes what was once considered fact is discovered to be false.

PTSD has been known by many names. In the early nineteenth century it was known as "Railway Spine," due to the large number of railroad collisions and the trauma that survivors suffered. In World War I, the symptoms of PTSD were referred to as "Shell Shock," which became "Combat Stress Reaction" (CSR) in World War II. The Vietnam War had such a large impact that the symptoms were classified as "Post-Vietnam Syndrome." Often whenever a soldier's struggle was mentioned in passing or generically described, people would say he had "Battle Fatigue." For Henry Rathbone and other Civil War vets, PTSD was known as "Soldier's Heart."[1]

Throughout history, soldiers have returned home from war battered physically, emotionally, and mentally. Although the physical injuries are the most obvious and get the most attention, the unseen damage to the mind is many times the worst scar of all. It can be argued that the prevalence of PTSD in the Civil War was greater and more extreme than in any U.S. war to follow. This is based not only on the fact that the Civil War holds the record for the most U.S. casualties, but also the severity of PTSD in the Civil War was intensified by the intimacy of the situation. Oftentimes soldiers were fighting and killing lifelong friends and family members. They watched as brothers, fathers, and uncles died beside them as they shot across enemy lines at their cousins and friends.

In addition, the destruction and loss of life was taking place on home soil. The collateral and incidental damage of the war was destroying their homes, towns, and way of life. When these soldiers finally returned home after the war or after being injured, it often was to a place they no longer recognized. This was particularly the case in the South. Fragile men with war torn minds and no support system attempted to rebuild a life that was not possible.

Another factor in the scope of PTSD was the age of the soldiers. According to Bell Irvin Wiley's book, *The Life of Billy Yank: The Common Soldier of the Union*, there were over 10,000 soldiers in the Union Army alone under the age of eighteen. Despite the official minimum enlistment age of eighteen, there were hundreds of young soldiers who were thirteen, fourteen, and fifteen.[2] The enlistment of young men wasn't solely the fault of recruiters, even though as the war progressed the age requirement was commonly overlooked. In fact, the recruiters had no way of verifying the age of the young men that valiantly stepped forward willing to fight and die for their cause.

What this meant was the war saw a plethora of young minds at the front lines of bloody battles. Most of these soldiers, including those who were eighteen and older, had limited life experience. They had little or no experience with death, mortality, and the grieving process. And with the war, they were thrust into scenes of gore, horror, and mass killing. This confluence of age, relation to the enemy, homeland proximity, and unpreparedness made the Civil War a perfect environment for PTSD to flourish.

In the modern medical world, new diseases consistently come to light as doctors and researchers learn more about the human mind. Through clinical and medical trials, science is able to gain deeper insight into the way people react to traumatic situations. Illnesses and diseases are classified as to the severity of symptoms, and many times these levels are given specific names to differentiate a patient's magnitude of symptoms.

Post-traumatic stress disorder is as old as human existence, but until relatively recently the illness was applied strictly to the effects of war or battle. This was due, in part, to how little psychology understood about traumatic situations. Practitioners and scientists didn't realize how wide reaching the symptoms of PTSD were. They also got a late start Post-traumatic stress disorder wasn't officially recognized as a distinct diagnosis until 1980. And even then it didn't gain a lot of initial traction. In England, the disorder was considered specific to the United States and Vietnam Veterans.[3] But the information, outlook, and veracity of focus on the disorder has increased vastly in the last ten years. So with a disorder officially only thirty-four years old, it's easy to understand why so much new information is being discovered every year. As with many illnesses, PTSD entails a spectrum. Doctors now realize the disorder doesn't solely result from war or battle, and it doesn't even have to spring from an act of violence. Any type of trauma, sudden or prolonged, can light the fuse of PTSD.

But what is trauma? What is traumatic to one person may not necessarily be traumatic to another. As Matthew J. Friedman, Ph.D., Professor of Psychiatry at Dartmouth, writes, "there are individual differences regarding the capacity to cope with catastrophic stress." In Friedman's article, *PTSD History and Overview*, he discusses the transformation in the understanding of PTSD. When PTSD was diagnosed in early patients, most physicians and researchers looked for patients that encountered a trauma or stressor that was beyond the normal "vicissitudes of life." However, psychologists soon realized that "normal" was a subjective term, and they began treating each case on its own merits.

They determined what was traumatic to each specific person, instead of labeling an event as a trauma. Looking beyond the "normal" was groundbreaking, as early post-traumatic diagnosis didn't include such everyday stressors as divorce, money problems, and prolonged illness. The thinking was that most people had the ability to deal with such stressors, but when faced with a clearly catastrophic trauma their mind would be overwhelmed. Now it's understood that the trauma can be a collection or aggregate of events and that there is no normal level of trauma. It's different for each person.

When analyzing post-traumatic stress disorder it's important to understand the base of the illness and where the symptoms stem from. PTSD as an illness falls under the umbrella of anxiety disorders. According to the National Institute of Mental Health, "anxiety is a normal reaction to stress and can actually be beneficial in some situations. For some people, however, anxiety can become excessive." Anxiety disorders are a family or collection of illnesses that involve similar traits and characteristics. Disorders such as obsessive-compulsive disorder, PTSD, and social anxiety all involve difficulty in controlling anxiety in specific situations. Sufferers are aware of what is happening, but they have little or no control over how they react.

Taking a closer look at the specific requirements of diagnosing post-traumatic stress disorder from the latest edition of the *Diagnostic and Statistical Manual of Mental Disorders*, it is clear that Henry Rathbone had the proper criteria necessary. When diagnosing a patient with PTSD, doctors evaluate a person based on eight criteria.

1. The stressor the person was exposed to involved death, threatened death or serious injury, or sexual violence.
2. The traumatic event is re-experienced through recurrent memories, nightmares, flashbacks, or prolonged distress.
3. The person avoids all trauma related thoughts or external reminders.
4. Negative changes in mood or memory following the event,

including negative beliefs about themselves or the world, distorted blame of self, feeling alienated from others.

5. At least two of the following alterations in arousal and reactivity after the traumatic event: Irritable or aggressive behavior, reckless behavior, hyper vigilance, exaggerated startle response, problems in concentration, sleep disturbance.
6. Symptoms must persist more than one month.
7. Significant symptom related distress or functional impairment in environments such as social or occupational.
8. Symptoms are not due to medication or substance abuse.[4]

Applying the first of the criteria to Henry, we can readily answer in the affirmative, whether in reference to the assassination or his war experiences.

The second criterion is many times referred to as "intrusive recollection" and refers to memories flooding back into the mind without warning, reason, or rational cause. The memories might return as nightmares or while daydreaming or having a connected stimuli stir up the entire traumatic narrative. In extreme cases, the patient may actually have a flashback and begin reenacting the trauma. In laboratories, researchers are able to use this criterion to elicit a response or trigger a PTSD reaction. By using images or items related to a patient's tragedy or stressor, they can provoke the patient into a state of stress.

Witnessing the death of Abraham Lincoln must have provided an endless deluge of stimuli. As noted earlier, there have been fifteen thousand books written about Lincoln. His popularity and celebrity have never dwindled over time, and in the decades after his death, his image, likeness, and words infuse the character of what it means to be American. Henry would never be able to escape reminders of that night. Even small things could take him back, such as a laugh from Clara that was reminiscent of a giggle she let out during *Our American Cousin*. If Henry went to another theater or simply passed one on the street, would the details of that night run through his mind? Reading the newspaper must have been especially difficult, as was overhearing friends or strangers discuss Lincoln.

Avoiding Abraham Lincoln was nearly impossible. Moving the family to Europe may have provided him some respite from living in Lincoln's shadow, as he was far less the celebrity there. Regardless of this, Henry had one reminder that followed him wherever he went: his oldest son, Henry Riggs Rathbone. Born on Lincoln's birthday, young Riggs no doubt elicited thoughts of the assassination.

The other reminder of Henry's inescapable sense of horror and failure was of course the large scar that ran from his elbow to his shoulder. Not only was the scar visible, but the nerve damage Henry incurred meant he would never regain full use or strength of his left arm. Thus even picking up one of his children was liable to inspire a twinge of guilt, regret, shame, anger, or sadness.

Avoiding Abraham leads into the symptom criterion of avoiding any stimuli that may be reminiscent of the traumatic event. As with most people, patients with post-traumatic stress guide their actions and life decisions in directions they believe will bring them into the least amount of contact with stimuli related to the trauma. They block out all connected stimuli both physically and mentally. Meaning they don't go to places where something might remind them of the trauma and they don't discuss anything that may lead down that path. They don't want to recognize any memories of the trauma because they can't deal with them. Patients simply strive to avoid an emotional response.

To cope with this, PTSD patients are able to disconnect their emotions from their intellectual reasoning. They focus only on what they deem reasonable, as emotions are a hindrance to them. Emotions will sabotage them. Because of this, PTSD sufferers are rarely able to engage in successful relationships. Henry dealt with this issue constantly. In the years following the assassination, Henry became less and less engaged—not just with Clara, but with friends and family members. This led to increased moodiness and erratic behavior, satisfying the fourth and fifth criteria.

According to friends and those who were especially intimate with Henry, after the assassination "he was noticed to be more depressed in manner and spirit than ever before; he was still a young man, but with a gravity greater than was natural for his years." They stated that there "was a cloud always hanging over the spirit of Rathbone."[5] It wasn't just Henry's mood, it was his actions as well. While he was known as mostly quiet and a devoted family man, he was also a "man subject to violent outburst of temper." This mix of devotion, anger, and confusion, led to anxiety and paranoid thoughts of jealousy. As noted by several sources, "whenever any gentleman, even a relative" approached Clara, Henry's jealous thoughts became uncontrollable. It was a trait that intensified over the years and became such an obsession with him that many friends considered him a "monomaniac on the subject."[6] Rathbone wasn't able to keep these outbursts private, and many close friends and family members were aware of the situation. According to one source, "when in an excited mood" he once threatened Clara's life.[7]

Criteria six and seven are easily observed and verified. The symptoms that Henry suffered from lasted much longer than a month. In fact, the symptoms seemed to progress slowly over time as the ruminations continued to eat away at him. Such a delayed onset of symptoms may demonstrate how valiantly Henry struggled to ward off the debilitating thoughts and regrets. Maybe he was able to busy his mind with enough distractions, such as marriage and children, to keep the horrible images at bay. But as those distractions blended into routine, the horrors of the assassination overtook his mind.

The last criterion, which states the symptoms are not due to medication or substance abuse, is difficult to completely ignore. There is no concrete evidence that points to overuse of drugs by Rathbone. But looking at the details of his life, there are clues that some drug use was possible. Rathbone suffered from severe dyspepsia. Enough so that he traveled to Europe in an attempt to discover new medicines and treatments. In his search for relief did he discover a drug that may have altered his perception of the world? During the late nineteenth century opiates were often prescribed to deal with ailments that could not be cured or properly treated by other means. These opiates were commonly abused, just as many prescription drugs are abused today. After all, it's valid for the human body to crave a substance that makes it feel better. There is no record of Rathbone taking any sort of opiate, but it cannot be ruled out.

One more item to discuss is the use of homeopathic drugs. The family doctor, G.W. Pope, was a homeopathic doctor and would have most likely prescribed the drug mercurius vivus for Rathbone's dyspepsia. Mercurius vivus was commonly taken for indigestion problems and still is in use today. Another name for the drug is Quicksilver, and the major ingredient is mercury. Although today's Quicksilver has such a diluted form of mercury it's not a valid concern, we can't determine the precise makeup of the Quicksilver that Henry may have taken. Mercury, as was the case with John Wilkes Booth's killer, John Corbett, has a negative effect on the mind. Long-time exposure to Mercury has been linked to symptoms such as depression and anxiety.

Now that all criteria have been reviewed and Henry Rathbone seems to satisfy all the symptoms for diagnosis of PTSD, we can look a little closer into why individuals suffer from it. Compared to other mental illnesses, PTSD is in a slightly different category, because part of its component lies with external events, rather than on internal abnormalities. Something has to cause a person to break down, which means it has to be big enough to shatter a person's threshold. While every person will have a different threshold for what their mind considers to be catastrophically traumatic, some events are seen as universally catastrophic. Events "such as rape, torture, genocide, and severe war zone stress" meet this universal threshold level.[8] It also stands to reason that there are different levels within these universal truths. And whereas it's true that PTSD is caused by external events, there is some evidence that specific individuals are predisposed to react to the same external events differently. Meaning they are genetically predisposed to suffer from post-traumatic stress disorder.

According to a study completed by the Semel Institute for Neuroscience and Human Behavior at UCLA, the likelihood of developing PTSD symptoms can be traced to specific variants of two genes, TPH1 and TPH2. The study, which was attempting to

The aftermath of the 1988 Spitak earthquake in Armenia.

understand why some victims give in to PTSD while others that experience the same trauma don't, turned their attention to the survivors of the 1988 Spitak earthquake in Armenia.

The damage from the earthquake was horrific and extensive, with the toll reaching 25,000 fatalities and approximately $14.2 billion in monetary damage.[9] Using this traumatic event as their starting point, the research team extracted the DNA of 200 adults, from several generations of twelve different families, all of which suffered PTSD symptoms related to the earthquake.[10] Their analysis showed that individuals with the specific variants of TPH1 and TPH2 were more prone to develop PTSD symptoms. The reasoning behind it was that TPH1 and TPH2 control serotonin levels and regulate mood, sleep, and alertness. These are all major components of PTSD.

Relating this to Henry Rathbone, it's possible to estimate that he was genetically susceptible to post-traumatic stress disorder. Unlike the earthquake research, however, there are no controls to compare Henry to, a crucial part of all scientific experimentation. He had a singular experience that night. Had there been another person who came into contact with John Wilkes Booth and let him go free, we could compare and contrast the two. But that isn't the case. Yes, Mary Todd Lincoln and Clara Harris lived through the event in very similar ways, but neither one was personally injured. And neither one attempted to detain the killer, nor came in contact with the killer. It was a very visceral experience, and Henry went through it completely alone.

We know that PTSD has both genetic and external factors, but the environment that a person grew up in also plays a large part. The developmental environment can provide learned behavior and create a foundation of trauma reaction that a person can reflect upon. The environment that Henry grew up in was far from adverse, and he faced very little trauma in comparison to most children of the nineteenth century. In fact, beyond the death of his father, it's difficult to find any aspect of his early life that put him in a disadvantaged situation.

Having said that, however, it's important to keep in mind each person's life experience is relative and specific to them. Everyone's struggle is subjective. Comparing two people's lives from an external point of view is futile. Everyone's issues and concerns are relative with respect to their way of life. The makeup of who we are as people, genetically and environmentally, creates how we view the world and how the events of life will impact us. For Henry Rathbone, his developmental environment, his genetic code, and the assassination all combined to form the necessary ingredients for his specific post-traumatic stress disorder. Henry was the only person in the world to face his situation, so there's no way to properly compare how someone else would react. Henry's life didn't prepare him for such a situation. For the majority of his life, especially after the assassination, Henry hid behind his wealth. He never had to overcome obstacles and put his past traumas aside to become a flourishing adult. He never grew from the experience and focused on the lessons learned. Perhaps it's because he couldn't. Perhaps he didn't have it in him, which wouldn't have been his fault. Perhaps his genetics would have worked against him regardless.

On the other side of the coin was Abraham Lincoln, who seemed to thrive on the stress he encountered throughout his entire life. He suffered through the death of his mother, the death of his first love, and multiple political defeats, yet he always arose from the ashes a stronger man. In 1862, after the death of his eleven-year-old son Willie, Abraham Lincoln carried the weight of many worlds, politically and personally. He was the main person in charge of keeping the United States together and yet he was making little ground on the cause. Thousands of men were dying from the choices he was making and the body count was growing fast. In addition to the constant pressures of the Presidency and the lost sons of America, he now had to mourn for his own boy. But he had to do it the only way Abraham Lincoln knew how.

He could not outwardly show his struggle, yet he wore it in the character evident on his face. Lincoln was the man that had to soldier on, pick up the pieces, and drive down the forces that would allow tragedy to prevail. He was the steadfast support that helped Mary Todd through Willie's death, and he was the rock that did not crumble under the weight of the Civil War. Abraham Lincoln did what he'd done his entire life and flourished in the face of opposition. Researchers now are discovering that this trait is not as uncommon as it may seem.

It's called post-traumatic growth. It is a new discovery, and the medical world is still uncovering its details through studies and research. Post-traumatic growth is exactly what it sounds like. The concept, according to the article *Post-Traumatic Growth: Conceptual Foundations and Empirical Evidence,* is the experience of positive change that occurs as a result of the struggle with highly challenging life crises. So the same tragedy may give rise for one person to PTSD and for another to growth. This growth can be seen in an increased appreciation for life, more meaningful relationships, increased personal strength, or changed life priorities. In a general sense, these individuals take traumatic or challenging experiences and internalize them, undergo the cycle of emotions and ultimately come out with a new perspective or understanding of themselves or the world around them.

Unfortunately for Henry and his family he was not able to find a silver lining in the assassination experience. This could be due to the specific nature of the event. Many of life's traumatic moments can be generalized or are common amongst most humans. The loss of loved ones, car accidents, war, divorce, and rape are all examples of horrible events that happen to many people each year. This provides an opportunity for people dealing with these events to compare them to others dealing with the same struggle. They can confide in others that understand what they are going through and look for answers and find comfort in the commonality of the situation. Henry Rathbone had nothing like this. There was no one who truly understood his pain.

What Henry experienced for the rest of his post-assassination life was a condition or symptom directly related to PTSD referred to as survivors guilt. Despite the fact that Henry wasn't there as an official body guard or protector of Lincoln, he still felt a sense of responsibility for the President's death. As Kathleen Nader, D.S.W., explains in her article *Guilt Following Traumatic Events*, one major reason for someone having perceived guilt after a traumatic event is the inability to have overcome "the bad guy."[11] In Rathbone's case, it was an actual bad guy, not a proverbial one. He faced the man head on, but lost in the end.

As we discussed earlier, whether Rathbone noticed Booth enter the President's box before the shot or after the shot could have an effect on the severity of the guilt Henry felt. Regardless of this, Henry was alive and Lincoln was not. This failure to protect may have haunted Henry as his family started growing. As a father, your purpose is to protect your family. Clara and his children were the most important things in his life, and he didn't want anything to happen to them. He wanted to protect them from their own tragedy, yet at the same time he had already failed once to protect the most important person in the world.

At the end of all analysis and postulating, the most important thing to glean is that the madness of Henry Rathbone is a lost lesson in the impact that trauma can have on the mind. No matter what the person's prior experiences are or what training he may have had, the human brain remains a great unknown. Henry's story is also a lost lesson on how small a person can feel after coming so close to greatness.

In any person's life, opportunity arrives in many ways, but it usually shows up unannounced. Whether it's opportunity to achieve success, such as at work or school, or opportunity to act in a specific way in the face of adversity, a person rarely gets a second chance. Those men and women throughout history who were able to take advantage of great opportunities are remembered for ages. They become myths and legends for later generations to read about and learn from. But what happens when you come face to face with a great opportunity and you fail to take advantage? And while the opportunity may have arrived unknowingly, upon reflection it's ascertained that the repercussions were tragic and monumental. How does that affect a person? The final tragedy of Henry Rathbone's life was that his story was forgotten, when we could have learned so much.

9

A Christmas Tragedy

Two days before Christmas, the Rathbone family was busy with holiday preparations. It was to be a wonderful Christmas with the three children, Henry Riggs, Gerald, and Pauline. They were thirteen, twelve, and eleven, respectively, and still young enough so that Christmas was a magical day. The anticipation of the holiday events was no doubt palpable, filling the house with high spirits. The only sour spot was the habitual poor mood of Henry.

His somberness cloaked the family in negativity. While he was overwhelmingly solemn as usual, Henry's depression and melancholy of the previous months sharply increased in the days leading up to Christmas. There was a noticeable change in his brooding. Henry was colder and more distant than normal. The new peculiarities of his mood did not go unnoticed by Clara and her sister. It was so evident that a few days before Christmas Eve, Clara remarked, "Well, the end is not far off."[1]

Clara expected that Henry would attempt suicide. Her husband's despondency evolved from the normal ups and downs. Now his depression was less of a passing mood and more like an aspect of his personality. The cycle of happy Henry and sad Henry abated as he finally completed his transformation, his mind succumbing to the preoccupation of worry and anxiety. His behavior was scattered, alternating between restlessness and bouts of foggy-mindedness. He was erratic and had regular outbursts. His dyspepsia and the incessant symptoms of the disease no doubt affected his mood. Clara made note of this in her letters back home after they reached Germany.[2]

Henry's recent actions caused Clara more concern than normal. Now more than ever, she feared for her safety, as well the safety of the children. Most of all she worried about Henry. He seemed different now than before they had left Albany nearly a year ago. Even at that time his actions were a cause for concern. Henry's behavior was so bizarre and possibly dangerous at the time that it sent up red flags among the Rathbone and Harris relatives in Albany. It was so distressing that they discussed with Clara the wisdom of allowing her to remain with Henry, asking that she entertain the idea of separating from him.[3]

Although it was an idea that was not common in the nineteenth century, Clara understood the concerns and weighed her options. While she may have hoped that Henry's moods were ultimately innocent and innocuous, there was an underlying profound discomfort. After much contemplation, her love for Henry won out. Clara decided her duty was to her husband and she stayed with him. It was her ultimate belief that she was living only so that she might watch over him.[4]

Clara loved Henry and couldn't leave him, but she understood she would need help, which is why she asked Louise to join them. Henry was probably aware that many discussions concerning his mental health had transpired, which only fueled the fire of his paranoia. Not only was Henry extremely and unjustifiably jealous of any attention shown to Clara, but now the Colonel became certain that his children would be taken away from him.

Henry was aware of the perception people had of him, and he heard the rumors and hushed murmurs around the house. He grew intensely wary of new people and "strange persons" he didn't know. He was "shy of human beings," his German neighbors stated.[5] Henry felt he had to be on guard at all times to prevent anything from happening to his wife or children. They were his to watch over and no one else could take them away. Henry slept with a loaded revolver under his pillow at night, a telltale sign that his paranoia and anxiety had gotten the better of him. He was not going to fall victim to a surprise attack again.

His diseased mind held sway, and he could no longer cope with the ruminations of that fateful April evening at Ford's Theatre. The pain and regret had fully evolved into an all-consuming haunting of his mind. The stress of his convoluted and imaginary concerns seeped into his everyday life decisions, causing him to fear the slightest possibilities as virtual certainties.

On Sunday, December 22, 1883, three days before Christmas, Henry sat alone at a drawing-room table in the Hanover home. Without a sound Henry separated himself from the rest of the family and filled his time by "staring blankly and picking at a handkerchief." The thoughts that echoed in his mind, over and over again, can only be imagined. Henry's latest concern must have been a great burden. He had convinced himself that Clara was leaving him and he wasn't sure how to stop it. He was convinced that when she left she would take the children with her. It was an idea that permeated his mind and could not be expelled. Regardless of any evidence to the contrary, Henry knew it as an absolute truth. He was certain that a plot was already underway and he needed be on his toes.

Henry trusted no one and judged that everyone was in collusion against him. Henry loved his children, and at no cost would he allow his children to be taken from him. Clara and the children were all he had. So there he sat alone in the drawing room, picking away at a handkerchief, Henry's mind oscillating from deep adoration of his family to hatred of an imaginary conspiracy. His ability to reason was crumbling with each passing moment. His fears were not completely without warrant, though. He knew Clara had discussed the possibility of leaving him, and that was enough for this thought to fester. Over the months it had grown into an all-consuming priority. Henry wasn't going to let it happen.

That night Henry slept poorly, a common symptom of dyspepsia sufferers, and no doubt his ruminations contributed to his insomnia. We can't know for sure if Henry tossed and turned, stayed awake all night, or woke up early, but at approximately 5:30 in the morning, December 23, he got up and left the bedroom.

He was fully dressed and carried a light in one hand and his revolver in the other. Moments later, just down the hall from Henry and Clara's room, a knock rattled the children's bedroom door. Clara's sister, Louise, shared the room with the children and rose from her bed to answer.

"Is Pauline in bed?" Henry asked.

"Yes," Louise answered from behind the door.

Rathbone's paranoia was at an all-time high. Henry envisioned the children dressed and ready to leave him. It was an image that enraged him further.

"Are the boys in their room?" Henry asked.

Louise responded in the affirmative, but kept the door closed. Clara, presumably woken by the noise in the hall, found Henry missing from the bed. She walked into the hall, and her fears mounted when she saw the revolver in her husband's hand. Clara's only goal at that moment was to protect her children and remove them from the path of her deranged husband.

"Open the door, I want to see them," Henry begged.

Louise cracked the door open, but Clara had reached Henry by that time.

"Dear husband, do calm yourself," Clara said.

Clara attempted to guide Henry back toward their bedroom, at the same time calling out to Louise.

"Lock the door and save the children; there is going to be dreadful work."

Reports state that upon hearing Clara's warning and the sound of the children's door locking, his passion exploded. He grabbed Clara by the arm and dragged her into their bedroom. Louise listened from the children's room down the hall. Sounds of a struggle resonated.

The door to Henry and Clara's bedroom was locked and unlocked three times. It's hard to say if Henry was trying to get to the children and Clara was preventing him, or if Clara was trying to escape and Henry was stopping her. The educated guess is the former scenario. While Clara was known to be "untiring in her devotion to her husband," the love of her children was greater. The struggle that morning was almost resoundingly due to Clara's attempt to quell any ill motives that Henry had toward her three little angels.

Down the hall in the children's room it isn't known if the children were awoken by the noises in their parent's room, but Louise was well aware. Wanting to do something to protect her sister, she left the children alone for a moment and made a futile attempt at calming the squall. Louise was able to enter the couple's room, but Henry quickly escorted her out and locked the door behind her. Not long after, Clara screamed.

"Henry, let me live!" echoed into the hall.[6]

Two gunshots rang out.

This was followed by haunting silence.

Moments later, Louise and a house servant who had heard the noise approached the locked bedroom door. The two of them broke through and found Clara sprawled on the bed.[7] She was enveloped in blood that poured from bullet and knife wounds. Clara received two bullets to the chest and a knife to her heart. As life seeped from her body, Clara's last vision was her sister's beseeching face at her side. Clara's last words were, "He has killed us both at last." She was dead within five minutes.

Henry was spread out on the floor next to the bed near a large porcelain stove. Next to him was "a six-shooter with three empty chambers and a dagger covered with gore."[8] Awake but delirious, he was also covered in blood. It wasn't Clara's blood, however, it was his own. After attacking Clara, Henry turned the knife on himself, inflicting five stab wounds, one that plunged all the way to his lung.

The shock and delirium that accompanied his horrendous act may have been the last straw for Henry's poor mind. Louise stood in horror near her murdered sister and watched as Henry begged her for a glass of brandy. He yelled out that he was severely injured while writhing in pain. Henry then called out

A National Police Gazette sketch of Henry Rathbone's murder of his wife, Clara.

for Clara. She was never going to answer, but Henry didn't know that. He had no memory of what had happened moments earlier. He was able to muster the strength to pull himself up to the bed, where he saw Clara's lifeless body. Taking in the morbid scene around him he dubiously asked Louise, "Who could have done this? I have no enemies!"[9]

Henry's mind simply didn't connect him to the crime.[10] Falling back to the ground and still conscious, Henry pleaded to be taken to the city hospital. Louise called for help and immediately notified the German police. On their arrival, the police stated Henry was adamantly warning them of men hiding behind the paintings on the bedroom walls. Henry was arrested and taken to receive medical attention for his wounds.

When the news of Clara's murder reached the United States it was received with a mix of shock and expectation. Most people in America treated the story of Henry as a man gone mad, a maniac who turned on the ones he loved. Henry's closest friends knew how much Henry loved Clara and the children, however, and they were surprised it had come to this. Hamilton Harris noted that he "never saw a man who gave more evidences of deeply loving his wife and children."[11] Henry's children and wife were those he loved most in the world. His entire life revolved around them. He had no interests outside of them.

According to relatives, you would always find him at home and never out at the clubs or calling upon acquaintances. His family was his life. In the end, this may have been a detriment to him. While being a devoted husband and father is a lovely trait, Henry needed a diversion. He had no job and no hobbies. He became obsessed with his family, particularly Clara, and when his fractured mind latched onto the possibility of losing that he took matters into his own unstable hands. It seems contradictory that someone who, according to neighbors, lived on the most affectionate terms with his family would resort to hurting them.[12] For a man whose family

Colonel William H. Harris. Clara's brother and Henry's step-brother. After Clara's death, the three Rathbone children went to live their uncle in Cleveland, Ohio.

remarked that no man ever loved a woman more devotedly than he did his wife to turn on her with knife and gun confounds the mind.[13] How could someone take the life of a loved one?

Colonel James G. Berret, Henry's attorney in Washington D.C., stated that, "I don't think that he ever recovered from the shock of the night in President Lincoln's box at the theatre. The scene always haunted his mind. He was at times subject to fits of despondency and moodiness." Dr. Pope pronounced the murder a case of sudden and acute homicidal mania, followed by long continued melancholia, which was the result of his chronic dyspepsia.[14] This was a popular view taken by friends and strangers alike. His involvement in the assassination was commonly noted in articles announcing Clara's death. A connection between the murder and Henry's failure to protect Lincoln was quickly made, and the case on Rathbone was all but closed.

Clara was buried on January 2, 1884, a little more than a week after her murder. According to newspapers it was largely attended by American and English friends of the family.[15] Clara and Louise's brother, Colonel William H. Harris, was the first member of the family to leave for Hanover. Coming from Cleveland he made a quick stop in Albany before boarding the Baltic and setting sail for Europe.[16] He met his sister Louise upon his arrival. She and the children had been living in the nearby Hotel Royal while the murder investigation took place.

Henry's trial was held in January 1884, but it did not last long. Henry claimed to have no memory of killing Clara. His defense was unchanged, as he continued to state that an intruder murdered his wife and attacked him. The German court stopped the trial when evidence was submitted "that he had shown symptoms of insanity at various times since Lincoln's death."[17] He was sentenced to an asylum for the criminally insane in nearby Hildesheim, Germany, where he would spend the remaining twenty-seven years of his life.

10
LIFE AND DEATH IN THE ASYLUM

The doors of St. Michael's Cathedral in Hildesheim, Germany are the essence of historical beauty. Over sixteen feet high, the bronze double doors are adorned with reliefs depicting the "Fall of Man" and the "Salvation of Man." Flowing in a U-shaped pattern and covering sixteen panels, eight panels on each door, the story begins at the top of the left door. The first four panels on the left side begin with the Genesis tale of Adam and Eve's progression to banishment. The bottom four panels of the left door give a pictorial explanation of Cain being cursed for the murder of his brother. On the right door, beginning from the bottom and moving up, the birth of Jesus Christ is presented. The final four panels, adorning the top of the right door, present the Passion and the Resurrection of Christ.

The Bernward Doors, as they are now referred to, came from the Cathedral's founder, Bishop Bernward, who had a deep love of art and architecture. It was among the majestic art and architecture of St. Michael's Cathedral and the adjoining Benedictine monastery that Henry Rathbone spent the remainder of his life. The monastery was the town's official asylum for the insane and provided a place for Henry to finally find some peace.

The Bernward Doors, and the stories they told, confronted Henry for the remainder of his life. The allegorical connections to the fall of man, the suffering of a martyr and a resurrection, undoubtedly sparked Henry's mind. Lincoln was the Christ of the United States. His death ensured he was a martyr for his cause and the South was soon to be reborn without slavery.

Hildesheim was, and still is, a town of many churches. The city is consistently lauded for its old world charm and as one of the most picturesque and beautiful in all Germany. This simple life provided Henry a world free of responsibility and the structure of the asylum provided a release from the demands of society. However, Henry's mind was altered forever now. He would never be anything like the man he was before. He now wandered the halls of the "Benedictine convent that once adjoined the church with cloistered walks."[1]

The church was rarely used during the time of the insane asylum, and many times the inmates used it as a sort of recreation center, sometimes using it to play a game of ninepins. St. Michael's church was also a popular tourist destination, even between 1884 and 1911 when Henry lived on the grounds. The unique art and architecture composed many must-see items for art students and admirers.

Interior of St. Michael's Cathedral.
Source: Nash's Pall Mall Magazine

In addition to the immense Bernward doors, St. Michael's crowning glory was the painted wooden ceiling of 1180, the only one of its kind north of the Alps. When visitors arrived to take in the painstaking details of Bernward's vision, they could hear the inmates of the asylum just outside the walls. One visitor noted it was an "uncanny experience to be dreaming alone in this church and to be roused by a sudden chorus of horrible laughter and heartrending shrieks from the insane in the adjoining cloisters. It is even more distressing to visit the cloisters and see the poor souls hurrying about distractedly among the foliage and flowers, without the least appreciation for the lovely arcades and portals where the late Romanesque is so happily fused with the early Gothic."[2]

St. Michael's Cathedral- Hildesheim, Germany.

The visitor was probably not referring to Henry. Although Henry stayed there long enough to make a few friends, he mostly kept to himself. His paranoia and hallucinations were still ever present, and Henry was wary with regard to those he allowed in his company. He refused to go out walking with the other gentlemen of the asylum and also refused to eat with them.[3] But Henry did take his walks, around the grounds, where an avenue of trees surrounded the walls of the asylum. He had a somewhat easy way of life in the asylum and was probably allowed more lenience than other inmates, due to his less severe nature. But Henry still had his problems.

In August of 1891, a physician for the city of Hildesheim, Dr. A. Rosenbach, was sent to the asylum on behalf of the United States Army. Henry's pension was set to go into effect, and the military needed a physical and assessment completed. Upon greeting Henry, Rosenbach noted that Henry had an earnest expression of face, was polite, formal in manner, and was dressed very carefully. The doctor first observed the normal diagnostics, such as his height, 181 centimeters, and his weight, 65 kilos, while also trying to probe into the nature of his mental illness. He wanted to obtain the veracity of Henry's disease.

One of the first things that jumps out from Dr. Rosenbach's report is that the "examination of the body didn't reveal any signs of disease." Not once does Rosenbach mention any signs of indigestion or dyspepsia. However, the signs of insanity are clearly present. Although the doctor states that the cause of the disease is unknown, it is his final opinion that Henry suffered from delusions of persecution and that his disease was incurable. This opinion came as a result of his observations, discussions with the asylum doctors, and an interview with Henry.

As Rosenbach attempted to gauge Henry and more deeply investigate his state of mind, Rathbone became very suspicious. He requested that his statements be kept secret, thinking that if his information fell into the wrong hands it would prove detrimental to him. During the conversation Henry's humor changed at irregular intervals. He complained of being persecuted and tortured in the past, and he stated that he heard persons gliding and rustling out in the corridor. Upon further questioning, Henry stated there was an apparatus of destruction in the wall, which was blowing injurious vapors into his head, causing him to suffer headaches. Whether he actually had headaches is not clear.

Most interestingly of all were the two items that Henry refused to discuss with Dr. Rosenbach. Henry avoided all conversation regarding the death of President Lincoln and Clara. These topics, it seemed, were either too difficult to discuss or subconsciously Henry had pushed them from his mind. Dredging them up would have been too painful and possibly shattered an already fragile psychological infrastructure.

After Rosenbach's examination was added to the pension records, Henry's pension remained approved and he continued receiving twelve dollars a month from the Army. At this point William Harris, Clara's brother, was in charge of Henry's affairs. He was also the guardian of his children. Henry Riggs, Gerald, and Pauline had returned with their uncle to his home in Cleveland, remaining in his custody until they reached adulthood.

In Dr. Rosenbach's report, Henry showed the "least longing for his children." Henry also seemed to take little interest in the outside world. This was in a sense only fair, as the outside world took little interest in him. Henry had very few visitors in the quarter century he spent in Hildesheim. But it was to be expected, as Henry was confined to a remote location in a foreign country. His brother, Jared Lewis Rathbone, was appointed U.S. Consul to Paris in 1887.[4] He may have taken the time to visit his brother after moving within a more manageable traveling distance. There is some record that William Harris did come to visit him at times as well.[5] Beyond this scant company, though, Henry had practically no other connections to his past.

This might have been beneficial to Henry. It may have been just what he needed. He couldn't stand the constant reminders of the assassination night and the most recent tragedy of Clara's death. The only way for him to have any existence was complete excommunication from his former life. As the years progressed and Henry's children got older they began to take over control of Henry's affairs.

In 1903, at the age of thirty-three, Henry's oldest son, Henry Riggs Rathbone, filed a petition in the Supreme Court of the District to be appointed committee and trustee of Henry's estate.[6] Henry Riggs was appointed ancillary committee a few days after filing. A few years later, Henry Riggs began selling off some of his father's old real estate. Most of the children lived lives away from D.C., except for Pauline, and they had little use for the properties of their father. So when businesses and buyers came calling for these properties, the children made sure to take advantage of the opportunities.[7]

In September 1910, Henry's health began deteriorating. Newspapers in the United States reported on his failing state and noted the physicians of the asylum didn't expect him to live very long.[8] He would live for nearly eleven more months. The articles dutifully referenced his connection to the Lincoln assassination and the murder of Clara, but they also expounded on the nature of Henry's mental state. The opinions on the veracity of Henry's illness were varied. Whereas some articles described Henry as completely mad and wasting away in a cloud of insanity, other stories hinted that he may have regained his sanity early on during his stay. They noted that Henry was possibly of sound

Henry Riggs Rathbone (1870 - 1928)
U.S. Congressman from Illinois (1923 - 1928)
The oldest son of Henry and Clara he shared a birth date with Abraham Lincoln.
Source: Library of Congress

mind, but was being held by the asylum as it was the easy thing to do. One newspaper even made a comparison between Henry and the events surrounding H.K. Thaw, stating that Henry's "case seems to be a duplicate of" Thaw's.[9]

Harry Kendall Thaw was a notorious New York playboy and a spoiled heir to a railroad and coal fortune. It was a fortune that Thaw did nothing to help produce or maintain. H.K. Thaw made extravagant use of this fortune, though, and spent night and day stacking up transgressions such as drug use, gambling, and even expulsion from Harvard University. During his time in New York, Thaw began a rivalry with Stanford White, a well-known businessman and architect. The rivalry with White intensified after multiple embarrassing public snubs of Thaw by White.

Thaw's hatred for White grew with each act of humiliation. The final straw was when his future wife, Evelyn Nesbit, declared that she had lost her virginity to Stanford White. In 1906, a year after his marriage to Nesbit, Thaw found his opportunity to exact his revenge. During a theater show taking place on the roof of Madison Square Garden, Thaw walked to within two feet of White and fired three shots from a pistol into White's face. Stanford White died instantly.

It's important to look into the events surrounding these two men and realize the similarities between H.K. Thaw and Henry Rathbone are few and far between. The original comparison comes from the assumption that Henry "recovered his reason" and regained his sanity, although the evidence and reports from the asylum prove Rathbone's mind to be far from reasonable. Dr. Rosenbach stated that Henry was incurable. And many others noted that Henry suffered from hallucinations until the day he died.

It's also important to note the details of the murders. The H.K. Thaw trial was the sensation of its time, the murder trial of the early century, and turned out to be one of the first times the use of temporary insanity was used as a defense in court. Thaw was a despicable man with a contemptible character. While Thaw may have been dealing with mental illness himself, the quality of his state of mind was commonly known to be good, both during the murder and after. The tales of the Thaw family using their great wealth and influence to manipulate the court system have been well documented, and H.K. Thaw has been accused of faking his insanity.

Henry Rathbone, on the other hand, was an accomplished man of education and military experience. While he may have used his family's wealth to coast the majority of his life, the validity of his mental illness cannot be questioned. Henry's murder of Clara was not an act of revenge, predicated upon a series of slights and bullying. He was a deeply diseased man, mentally and physically, who never came to terms with those thirty seconds on April 14, 1865. It was not an act Henry put on to avoid imprisonment, like Thaw did. Henry was already imprisoned in his own mind. After being unable to escape those thoughts, he freed himself the only way he could — by destroying the two things still connecting him to Lincoln's assassination: his wife Clara and his memories.

On August 14, 1911, Henry died of unknown causes. He was seventy-four and had been ill for some time. It seemed that his body finally succumbed to his mind's wishes. Upon his death, Rathbone left an estate valued at $70,870 to his three children. Each child received $23,623 and his oldest son, Henry, was to be the administrator.[10] It was the farewell gift from a father they barely knew. All three children went on to become successful in their own right. The oldest, Henry Riggs Rathbone, the son born on Lincoln's Birthday, became a U.S. Congressman for the state of Illinois.

The death of Henry Reed Rathbone formed a fitting parallel to the manner of his involvement at Lincoln's assassination. Henry simply disappeared. After his death several obituaries ran the story in the United States, all of which recounted his attendance at Ford's Theatre, and many of the articles expounded on the reason behind his assignment to the asylum in Germany and the murder of Clara. The articles were short and to the point. They provided recollections of a former American soldier, a man present at the great 1865 tragedy, and an insane murderer — three basic classifications of Henry Rathbone.

Abraham Lincoln, the Martyr, Victorious- John Sartain 1865
This image shows the effect the assassination had on Lincoln's image.
George Washington welcoming Abraham into heaven is symbolic of the
equal status they shared after Lincoln's death.
Source: Library of Congress

From a bird's eye view those classifications are accurate enough, but in trying to understand those connotations more deeply we find there is much beneath the labels. Looking deeper into the life of Henry Rathbone we find a husband, a father, a friend, a sufferer, and a lost soul. Through investigation we determine that a strange set of coincidences pushed Rathbone to inhabit the unfortunate role he will forever play in American history. It seems Henry was destined to witness to the murder of Abraham Lincoln, a man whose equal is hard to be found.

This point cannot be emphasized too strongly. Lincoln was so revered that upon his death he was placed on a pedestal next to George Washington, the General of the American Revolution. Washington set many a precedent for what we know as moral truth, and he was a stoic American figure whose duties, actions, and wisdom had been vetted for nearly one hundred years. President Lincoln was able to attain that stature almost immediately. His guidance through America's worst war and his steadfast belief that the United States must remain intact made such an indelible mark on a country's people that he became an instant legend. As historians and researchers separate the man from the myth, Lincoln's wisdom, political intellect, and leadership has only grown in significance. While the details surrounding his death undoubtedly impacted his martyrdom, it's important to fully grasp this notion to completely understand the monumental sense of regret that Rathbone embodied. And if the unique contempt for oneself that Rathbone carried inside him can teach us anything, it is that greatness and failure must find a way to coexist. Unfortunately for Henry, the world of medicine wasn't able to give him any reprieve from the burden he carried. But his story can provide an example for others dealing with mental disorders. We can learn from the madness of Henry Rathbone.

A Message About Post-Traumatic Stress Disorder

In today's world, the recent advancements in medicine and research have greatly improved the quality of assistance that individuals that suffer from PTSD can receive. Unlike Henry Rathbone, patients today have many outlets that offer different kinds of help. From individual therapy, group sessions and prescription drugs there is a wide variety of assistance that people can try.

Whether someone is formally diagnosed with PTSD or thinks they may have the disorder, it's important to get treatment. Having a support system or even a single doctor that understands the symptoms they are facing can make a world of difference.

It's important for those that suffer from PTSD to understand they are not alone. In fact, PTSD falls into the category of an anxiety disorder and these disorders are the most common psychiatric illnesses affecting children and adults today. According to the Anxiety and Depression Association of America (ADAA), an estimated 40 million American adults suffer from anxiety disorders and only about one-third of those receive any treatment.

Remember that PTSD can start at any time. Sometimes the symptoms will begin immediately after a traumatic event, but the disorder can also take months or even years to start showing up. This is why it's important to get treatment. You may not be able to fully connect the feelings you're having to an event that happened years earlier. The correlation can many times be difficult to see by yourself. The symptoms may also stem from a combination of events and add up over time, resulting in thoughts and emotions that are difficult to bear.

PTSD and similar anxiety disorders are highly treatable. If you or someone you know may be dealing with symptoms of this disorder, please take the appropriate steps to receive the proper treatment. A good place to start is by talking with your doctor or a mental health care professional. You can also start the process by learning more about PTSD through either the Anxiety and Depression Association of America or the National Center for PTSD.

Take a lesson from the life of Henry Rathbone and use the advantages of the medical advances available to us today. There's no reason anyone has to suffer the way Henry, Clara and their children did.

Anxiety and Depression Association of America
www.adaa.org
240-485-1001

National Center for PTSD
www.ptsd.va.gov
Veterans Crisis Line: 1-800-273-8255

Appendix A
Capt. Matthew Blunt's Official Report From Antietam

CAMP NEAR SHARPSBURG,

September 25, 1862.

Lieutenant WILLIAM H. POWELL,
Acting Asst. Adjt. General, First Brigade, Regular Infantry.

SIR: Having been ordered to report on the operations of the
First Battalion Twelfth U. S. Infantry, since leaving Middletown
on the 15th, I have the honor to state that we continued our march,
crossing the range of mountains (Blue Ridge) by South Mountain
Pass over the battle-field of the previous day. After going through
the pass, General Sykes' division took up the advance, Colonel
Buchanan's brigade leading. We followed the enemy, and came
up which a short time before sunset, our batteries exchanging
shots with theirs, and their rear-guard (infantry) showing itself,
to dissolve as we advanced. This was kept up until dark, when
the enemy had crossed the bridge over Antietam Creek, on the
Baltimore turnpike. On the following day (16th) our artillery
engaged that of the enemy, who shelled our brigade considerably.
At 5 p.m. on the 16th the battalion was ordered to relieve the

Fourth Infantry in guarding the bridge over Antietam Creek, which it did until about 12 m. on the following day (17th), when the tide of battle uncovering the country on the other side of the bridge, our horse artillery and cavalry crossed the bridge at a gallop. The enemy opened a very heavy fire of artillery on the artillery and cavalry crossing the bridge, from which we lost 1 wounded (enlisted man). The sharpshooters of the enemy annoying Captain Tidball's battery. General Pleasonton asked me to advance a line of skirmishers to drive them back, which was immediately done under commanded of Captain Winthrop. Shortly after, General Sykes ordered the battalion to advance as a support to Tidball's battery. This was done, skirmishers being thrown out to the left of the battery.

The regular infantry on the field was at this time under the command of Captain Dryer, Fourth Infantry.

I received no further orders during the rest of the afternoon, and remained in the position assigned me until ordered to join the brigade at about 7 p.m. Our loss was 1 killed and 3 wounded.

The following officers were present guarding the bridge, and afternoon on skirmish duty or supporting Tidball's battery: Captain M. M. Blunt, commanding battalion; Captain H. R. Rathbone, acting field officer, commanding Company C; Captain William Sergeant, commanding Company F; Captain Francis Wister, commanding Company G; Captain F. Winthrop, commanding Company B; First Lieutenant M. H. Stacey, battalion adjutant; Second Lieutenant J. A. Duvillard, commanding Company H; Second Lieutenant T. H. Evans, commanding Company D; Second Lieutenant E. C. Allen, commanding Company A; Second Lieutenant T. D. Urmston; Second Lieutenant R. H. Pond, commanding Company E. Acting Assistant Surgeon Grant attended the battalion.

I am, sir, respectfully, your obedient servant,
M. M. BLUNT,
Captain Twelfth Infantry, Commanding First Battalion.

Appendix B
Testimony of
Major Henry R. Rathbone
For the Prosecution -
May 15, 1865

On the evening of the 14th of April last, at about twenty minutes past 8 o'clock, I, in company with Miss Harris, left my residence at the corner of Fifteenth and H Streets, and joined the President and Mrs. Lincoln, and went with them in their carriage, to Ford's Theater, on Tenth Street. On reaching the theater, when the presence of the President became known, the actors stopped playing, the band struck up "Hail to the Chief," and the audience rose and received him with vociferous cheering. The party proceeded along in the rear of the dress-circle and entered the box that had been set apart for their reception. On entering the box, there was a large arm-chair that was placed nearest the audience, farthest from the stage, which the President took and occupied during the whole of the evening, with one exception, when he got up to put on his coat, and returned and sat down again. When the second scene of the third act was being performed, and while I was intently observing the proceedings upon the stage, with my back toward the door, I heard the discharge of a pistol behind me, and, looking round, saw through the smoke a man between the door and the President. The distance from the door to where the President sat was about four feet. At the same time I heard the man shout some word, which I thought was "Freedom!" I instantly sprang toward him and seized him. He wrested himself from my grasp, and made a violent thrust at my breast with a large knife. I parried the blow by striking it up, and received a wound several inches deep in my left arm, between the elbow and the shoulder. The orifice of the wound was about an inch and a half in length, and extended upward toward the shoulder several inches. The man rushed to the front of the box, and I endeavored to seize him again, but only caught his clothes as he was leaping over the railing of the box. The clothes, as I believe, were torn in the attempt to hold him. As he went over upon the stage, I cried out, "Stop that man." I then turned to the President; his position was not changed; his head slightly bent forward, and his eyes were closed. I saw that he was unconscious, and, supposing him mortally wounded, rushed to the door for the purpose of calling medical aid.

On reaching the outer door of the passage way, I found it barred by a heavy piece of plank, one end of which was secured in the wall, and the other resting against the door. It had been so securely fastened that it required considerable force to remove it. This wedge or bar was about four feet from the floor. Persons upon the outside were beating against the door for the purpose of entering. I removed the bar, and the door was opened. Several persons, who represented themselves as surgeons, were allowed to enter. I saw there Colonel Crawford, and requested him to prevent other persons from entering the box.

I then returned to the box, and found the surgeons examining the President's person. They had not yet discovered the wound. As soon as it was discovered, it was determined to remove him from the theater. He was carried out, and I then proceeded to assist Mrs. Lincoln, who was intensely excited, to leave the theater. On reaching the head of the stairs, I requested Major Potter to aid me in assisting Mrs. Lincoln across the street to the house where the President was being conveyed. The wound which I had received had been bleeding very profusely, and on reaching the house, feeling very faint from the loss of blood, I seated myself in the hall, and soon after fainted away, and was laid upon the floor. Upon the return of consciousness I was taken to my residence.

In a review of the transactions, it is my confident belief that the time which elapsed between the discharge of the pistol and the time when the assassin leaped from the box did not exceed thirty seconds. Neither Mrs. Lincoln nor Miss Harris had left their seats.

(A bowie-knife, with a heavy seven-inch blade, was exhibited to the witness, stains of blood being still upon the blade.)

This knife might have made a wound similar to the one I received. The assassin held the blade in a horizontal position, I think, and the nature of the wound would indicate it; it came down with a sweeping blow from above.

(The knife was offered in evidence.)

Appendix C
The Wrong Clara

This image, consistently notated as Clara Harris, is not the
Clara Harris married to Major Rathbone. It's the same image
that was mistakenly displayed in Ford's Theatre for many years
and continues to be referenced as Clara. One item of note is the
wedding ring on the left hand of the woman pictured. Clara Harris
was not married on the reported date this picture was taken.

References

Introduction

1. "Those who misquote George Santayana are condemned to paraphrase him." NowPublic.com. <http://www.nowpublic. com/those-who-misquote-george-santayana-are-condemned-paraphrase-him#ixzz2LHKlv35u> (accessed February 12, 2011).

2. NPR Staff. "Forget Lincoln Logs: A Tower Of Books To Honor Abe." NPR. <http://www.npr.org/2012/02/20/147062501/ forget-lincoln-logs-a-tower-of-books-to-honor-abe> (accessed May 21, 2012).

3. POKORSKI, DOUG. "Lincoln-era assassination image was bogus." *The State Journal-Register* (Springfield), April 9, 2000. <http://www.newsbankschools.com/schools/pdf/Lincoln-era. pdf> (accessed August 21, 2012).

CHAPTER ONE

1. Cemetery, Engsohde. Interview by Eva Lennartz. Email interview. Engsohde Cemetery, June 3, 2013.

2. IBID

3. Ford's Theatre Museum Information Pamphlet.

4. Bumpus, T. Francis. "Chapter IX." In *The Cathedrals and Churches of the Rhine and North Germany,*. New York: J. Pott & Co., 1906. 266.

5. Baedeker, Karl. *Northern Germany, as Far as the Bavarian and Austrian Frontiers: Handbook for Travellers.* 14th rev. ed. Leipsic: K. Baedeker, 1904.

6. "A Teacher's Notes: Hildesheim and Harzburg." *Friends' Intelligencer* 52 (1895): 526-527.

7. Claussen, Martin Paul. *The Journal of the Senate, Including the Journal of the Executive Proceedings of the Senate.* Wilmington, Del.: Michael Glazier, 1977.

8. *Times-Union,* Cecil R. Roseberry, staff writer, April 16, 1961- A Tragedy That Blighted 2 More Lives.

9. Pension Evaluation Letter from Dr. A. Rosenbach, Oct. 13, 1891; Federal Military Pension Application- Civil War and Later Complete; National Archives Building, Washington, D.C.

10. Emerson, Jason. "Mrs. Lincoln Admitted Today." In *The Madness of Mary Lincoln.* Carbondale: Southern Illinois University Press, 2007. 66.

11. Furgurson, Ernest. "The Man Who Shot the Man Who Shot Lincoln." The American Scholar:. <http://theamericanscholar. org/the-man-who-shot-the-man-who-shot-lincoln/#. UW7tX7VQH5g> (accessed May 12, 2011).

12. Shorter, Edward. *A History of Psychiatry: From the Era of the Asylum to the Age of Prozac.* New York: John Wiley & Sons, 1997.

13. Noll, Richard. 2000. *The Encyclopedia of Schizophrenia and Other Psychotic Disorders*. New York, NY: Facts On File.

14. *The Daily Dispatch* (Richmond), "Mrs. Rathbone's Fate," January 2, 1884.

15. Rathbone, Henry. Interview with A.B. Olin. *Reminiscences and Souvenirs of the Assassination of Abraham Lincoln*. Wasington: Press of Rufus H. Darby, 1894. 73-76.

16. IBID

CHAPTER TWO

1. Reynolds, Cuyler. *Albany Chronicles, A History of the City Arranged Chronologically, from the Earliest Settlement to the Present Time*; illustrated with many historical pictures of rarity and reproductions of the Robert C. Pruyn collection of the mayors of Albany, owned by . Albany, N.Y.: J.B. Lyon Co., printers, 1906.

2. Talcott, S. V.. *Genealogical Notes of New York and New England Families*. Baltimore: Genealogical Pub. Co., 1973.

3. Rathbun, Frank H. . "Rathbones of Albany, N.Y., Achieved Wealth and Fame." *The Rathbun-Rathbone-Rathburn Family Historian* Eight, no. Three (1988).<http://www.michaelrathbun. org/08-1988/08-003.pdf> (accessed June 23, 2012).

4. IBID

5. Reynolds, Cuyler. *Albany Chronicles, A History of the City Arranged Chronologically, from the Earliest Settlement to the Present Time*; illustrated with many historical pictures of rarity and reproductions of the Robert C. Pruyn collection of the mayors of Albany, owned by . Albany, N.Y.: J.B. Lyon Co., printers, 1906.

6. IBID

7. *The Albany Lumber Trade, Its History and Extent*. Albany [N.Y.: Argus Co., printers, 1872.

8. "Population of the 90 Urban Places: 1830." Census.gov. <http://www.census.gov/population/www/documentation/ twps0027/tab06.txt> (accessed August 11, 2011).

9. *A Chronological History of Electrical Development from 600 B.C. ...* New York, N.Y.: National Electrical Manufacturers Association, 1946.

10. Lewis, Tom. *The Hudson a History*. New Haven: Yale University Press, 2005.

CHAPTER THREE

1. Reynolds, Cuyler. *Albany Chronicles, A History of the City Arranged Chronologically, from the Earliest Settlement to the Present Time*; illustrated with many historical pictures of rarity and reproductions of the Robert C. Pruyn collection of the mayors of Albany, owned by . Albany, N.Y.: J.B. Lyon Co., printers, 1906.

2. Albany Cemetery Internment Card- Cause of Death.

3. Fitzgerald, Edward. *A Hand Book for the Albany Rural Cemetery with an Appendix on Emblems*. Albany [N.Y.: Van Benthuysen Print. House, 1871.

4. *New York Tribune* (New York), "Colonel Rathbone's Mania: What Hamilton Harris Says," December 31, 1883.

5. Samuel H. Williamson, "Seven Ways to Compute the Relative Value of a U.S. Dollar Amount, 1774 to present," MeasuringWorth, April 2013.

6. Goodman, Ph.D., Robin F. , and Anita Gurian, Ph.D.. "About Posttraumatic Stress Disorder (PTSD)." American Academy of Experts in Traumatic Stress. <http://www.aaets.org/article147.htm> (accessed July 12, 2011).

7. IBID

8. "Cortland Observer." Cortland County Marriages. <http://www.usgenweb.info/nycortland/vitals/co182529.htm> (accessed February 8, 2012).

9. Hough, Franklin Benjamin. *The New York Civil List: Containing the Names and Origin of the Civil Divisions, and the Names and Dates of Election or Appointment of the Principal State and County Officers from the Revolution to the Present Time*. Albany, N.Y.: Weed, Parsons and Co., 1857.

10. Reynolds, Cuyler. *Albany Chronicles, A History of the City Arranged Chronologically, From the Earliest Settlement to the Present Time*; illustrated with many historical pictures of rarity and reproductions of the Robert C. Pruyn collection of

the mayors of Albany, owned by . Albany, N.Y.: J.B. Lyon Co., printers, 1906.

11. Goodwin, Hermon Camp. *Pioneer History, or, Cortland County and the Border Wars of New York: From the Earliest Period to the Present Time.* New York: A.B. Burdick, Publisher, 1859.

12. *Documents of the convention of the state of New York,* 1867-'68. Albany [N.Y.: Weed, Parsons and Co., 1868.

13. *New York Herald,* "Ira Harris Obituary" December 3, 1875.

14. Ham, Thomas H.. *A Genealogy of the Descendants of Nicholas Harris, M.D., Fifth in Descent from Thomas Harris of Providence, R.I., and Sketches of the Harris and the Following Families Connected by Marriage,* Tew, Hopkins, Smith, Arnold, Tibbits, Waterman, Olney, Williams,. Albany, N.Y.: [C.I.F. Ham], 1904.

15. Henry, Guy Verner. *Military record of civilian appointments in the United States Army.* New York: Carleton [etc., 1869.

16. Report from Schaffer Library, May 8, 1940, Union College. Schenectady, New York.

17. Letter from the Collections of Schaffer Library, May 13, 1940, Union College. Schenectady, New York.

18. IBID

19. Howell, George Rogers, and Jonathan Tenney. *Bi-centennial history of Albany history of the county of Albany, N.Y., from 1609 to 1886.* New York: W.W. Munsell & Co., 1886.

20. *New York Tribune* (New York), "Colonel Rathbone's Mania: What Hamilton Harris Says," December 31, 1883.

21. Report from Schaffer Library, May 8, 1940, Union College. Schenectady, New York.

22. Letter from the Collections of Schaffer Library, May 13, 1940, Union College. Schenectady, New York.

CHAPTER FOUR

1. "1860 Directory for City of Elmira, Chemung County, NY."
1860 Directory for City of Elmira, Chemung County, NY.
<http://www.joycetice.com/director/1860p155.htm> (accessed
June 28, 2013).

2. *Annual Report of the Adjutant General of the State of New York.*
Albany: C. VAN BENTHUYSEN, 1860.

3. "Delavan House was crowded to suffocation during the
entire   evening."   <(http://myloc.gov/exhibitions/Lincoln/
interactives/1861/html/feb_18/pdf/500j.pdf)>.

4. Thomas, Benjamin Platt. *Abraham Lincoln: a Biography.* [1st ed.
New York: Knopf, 1952.

5. Deusen, Glyndon G.. "The House Divided." In *Thurlow Weed,
Wizard of the Lobby.* Boston: Little, Brown and Co., 1947. 264.

6. Turner, Justin G., Linda Levitt Turner, and Mary Todd Lincoln.
Mary Todd Lincoln: her life and letters. [1st ed. New York: Knopf,
1972.

7. Basler, Roy P. "Letter to Simon Cameron." In *The Collected
Works of Abraham Lincoln;* volume 4: 1860-1861. Collector's ed.
Norwalk, Connecticut: The Easton Press, 1993. 387.

8. In *List of Cadets Admitted into the United States Military Academy,
West Point, N.y From Its Origin Till September 1, 1901* : with
tables exhibiting the results of examinations for admission,
and the corps to which the graduates have been promoted..
Washington: G.P.O., 1902. 79.

9. Beaudry, Louis N.. *Historic Records of the Fifth New York
Cavalry, First Ira Harris Guard: Its Organization, Marches, Raids,
Scouts Engagements and General Services, During the Rebellion of
1861-1865.* 2d ed. Albany, N.Y.: S.R. Gray, 1865.

10. Henry, Guy Verner. *Military Record of Civilian Appointments in
the United States Army.* New York: Carleton [etc., 1869.

11. Encyclopedia Britannica. "Seven Days' Battles (American
Civil War)." Encyclopedia Britannica Online. <http://www.

britannica.com/EBchecked/topic/536437/Seven-Days-Battles>
(accessed September 15, 2013).

12. Ruane, Michael. *Civil War Stories a 150th Anniversary Collection.*
New York: Diversion Books, 2013.

13. National Parks Service. "Casualties of Battle." National Parks
Service. <http://www.nps.gov/anti/historyculture/casualties.
htm> (accessed February 14, 2013).

14. Battlefield marker: Located on the south side of the Boonsboro
Pike, east of Rodman Avenue.

15. Scott, Robert N., H. M. Lazelle, George B. Davis, Leslie J.
Perry, Joseph W. Kirkley, Fred C. Ainsworth, John S. Moodey,
and Calvin D. Cowles. *The War of the Rebellion: A Compilation
of the Official Records of the Union and Confederate Armies.*
Washington, D.C.: Govt. Print. Off., 1880. Print.

16. Civil War Trust. "Fredericksburg." Civil War Trust.
<http://www.civilwar.org/battlefields/fredericksburg.
html?tab=facts> (accessed September 7, 2012).

17. Ruane, Michael. *Civil War Stories a 150th Anniversary Collection.*
New York: Diversion Books, 2013.

18. Basler, Roy P. "Letter to Edwin M. Stanton." In *The Collected
Works of Abraham Lincoln* ; volume 4: 1860-1861.. Collector's
Ed. Norwalk, Connecticut: The Easton Press, 1993. 387.

19. Brown, Dee Alexander. "Bloody Year on the Plains." *The
Galvanized Yankees.* Urbana: University of Illinois Press, 1963.
13-15. Print.

20. Scott, Robert N., H. M. Lazelle, George B. Davis, Leslie J.
Perry, Joseph W. Kirkley, Fred C. Ainsworth, John S. Moodey,
and Calvin D. Cowles. *The War of the Rebellion: A Compilation
of the Official Records of the Union and Confederate Armies.*
Washington, D.C.: Govt. Print. Off., 1880. Print.

CHAPTER FIVE

1. Ford's Theatre. "Explore Lincoln: Learn the Story." Ford's Theatre. <http://www.fordstheatre.org/sites/default/files/ ExploreLincoln.pdf> (accessed May 12, 2012).

2. Grant, Ulysses S., and E. B. Long. *Personal Memoirs of U.S. Grant.* New York, N.Y.: Da Capo Press, 1982. Print.

3. Oates, Stephen B.. *With Malice Toward None: The Life of Abraham Lincoln.* New York: Harper & Row, 1977. Print.

4. "Family: Mary Todd Lincoln." Mr. Lincoln's White House. N.p., n.d. Web. 12 Aug. 2012. <http://www.mrlincolnswhitehouse. org/inside.asp?ID=15&subjectID=2>.

5. Purcell, L. Edward. "Schuyler Colfax." *Vice Presidents.* New York: Infobase Pub., 2010. 168. Print.

6. Strecker, Trey. "Chapter One." *Dead Balls and Double Curves: An Anthology of Early Baseball Fiction.* Carbondale: Southern Illinois University Press, 2004. 24. Print.

7. Chambrun, Adolphe de Pineton, and Marie Hélène Marthe de Corcelles Chambrun. *Impressions of Lincoln and the Civil War, a foreigner's account;.* New York: Random House, 1952. Print.

8. Nicolay, John G.. *A Short Life of Abraham Lincoln: Condensed from Nicolay & Hay's Abraham Lincoln : A History.* New York: Century, 1902. Print.

9. Oates, Stephen B.. *With Malice Toward None: The Life of Abraham Lincoln.* New York: Harper & Row, 1977. Print.

10. Crook, W. H., and Margarita Spalding Gerry. "A new phase of the assassination." *Through Five Administrations; Reminiscences of Colonel William H. Crook, Body-Guard to President Lincoln,.* New York: Harper & Bros., 1910. 67. Print.

11. Bates, David Homer. "The Assassination." *Lincoln in the telegraph office recollections of the United States Military Telegraph Corps during the Civil War. Lincoln:* University of Nebraska Lincoln, 1995. 366-368. Print.

12. Bishop, Jim. *The Day Lincoln Was Shot.* New York: Harper, 1955.

13. IBID

14. Martin, Paul. "Lincoln's Missing Bodyguard." Smithsonian Magazine. N.p., 8 Apr. 2010. Web. 11 Dec. 2013. <http://www. smithsonianmag.com/history-archaeology/Lincolns-Missing-Bodyguard.html?c=y&page=1>.

15. Holzer, Harold. "Eyewitnesses Remember The "Fearful Night"." *Civil War Times* Apr. 1993: 12. Print.

16. "Frequently Asked Questions." National Parks Service. National Parks Service, 17 Dec. 2013. Web. 12 Oct. 2011. <http://www.nps.gov/foth/faqs.htm>.

17. "Lincoln's Last Day." National Parks Service. National Parks Service, 2 Dec. 2002. Web. 15 Oct. 2011. <http://www.nps.gov/ history/history/online>.

18. Fleming, Candace. *The Lincolns: A Scrapbook Look at Abraham and Mary.* New York: Schwartz & Wade Books, 2008. Print.

19. "Mary Todd Lincoln's Agony." Abraham Lincoln's Assassination. <http://rogerjnorton.com/Lincoln62.html> (accessed June 1, 2012).

20. Olszewski, George J.. *Restoration of Ford's Theatre, Washington D.C.* Washington, D.C.: U.S. Dept. of the Interior, National Park Service, National Capital Region :, 1963. Print.

21. Sandburg, Carl. *Abraham Lincoln.* Sangamon ed. New York: C. Scribner's, 1939. Print.

22. Olszewski, George J.. *Restoration of Ford's Theatre, Washington D.C..* Washington, D.C.: U.S. Dept. of the Interior, National Park Service, National Capital Region :, 1963. Print.

23. IBID

24. "A Tragedy That Blighted 2 More Lives." *Times-Union* [Albany] 16 Apr. 1961: -. Print.

25. Rathbone, Henry. Interview with A.B. Olin. Reminiscences and Souvenirs of the Assassination of Abraham Lincoln. Washington: Press of Rufus H. Darby, 1894. 73-76.

26. Filichia, Peter. "STAGESTRUCK by Peter Filichia: *Our American Cousin* - Playbill.com." Playbill. N.p., 15 Apr. 1998. Web. 23 Dec. 2013. <http://www.playbill.com/news/article/38244-STAGESTRUCK-by-Peter-Filichia-Our-American-Cousin>.

27. "Visible Proofs: Forensic Views of the Body: Galleries: Cases: The autopsy of President Abraham Lincoln." U.S National Library of Medicine. U.S. National Library of Medicine, 22 Nov. 2013. Web. 9 Apr. 2012. <http://www.nlm.nih.gov/visibleproofs/galleries/cases/lincoln.html>.

28. Rathbone, Henry. Interview with A.B. Olin. Reminiscences and Souvenirs of the Assassination of Abraham Lincoln. Washington: Press of Rufus H. Darby, 1894. 73-76.

29. The Whitesville News, "THE MURDER OF LINCOLN," January 1, 1895.

30. IBID

31. Reck, W. Emerson. "It Is Impossible For Him To Recover." A. Lincoln, His Last 24 Hours. Jefferson, N.C.: McFarland, 1987. 114. Print.

32. Rathbone, Henry. Interview with A.B. Olin. Reminiscences and Souvenirs of the Assassination of Abraham Lincoln. Washington: Press of Rufus H. Darby, 1894. 73-76.

33. Report of Dr. Charles A. Leale on Lincoln Assassination. Record Group 112: Office of the Surgeon General (War), 1775-1959, Entry 12, Letters Received, 1818-1889, National Archives Building, Washington, D.C.

34. "The assassination of Abraham Lincoln." The assassination of Abraham Lincoln. Friends of The Lincoln Collection of Indiana, Inc., n.d. Web. 12 Aug. 2012. <http://archive.org/stream/assassinationofarealinc#page/n13/mode/2up>.

35. IBID

36. "President Lincoln - The Tragedy." The Public Ledger [Philadelphia] 5 May 1865: n. pag. The Public Ledger - May 5, 1865. Web. 11 Aug. 2010.

CHAPTER SIX

1. Herold, David E., and Benjamin Perley Poore. *The Conspiracy Trial for the Murder of the President and the Attempt to Overthrow the Government by the Assassination of its Principal Officers.* Buffalo, NY: William S. Hein & Co., 2010. Print.

2. *Troy Daily Times,* "Col. Rathbone' s Terrible Deed—Particulars of the Tragedy – An Insane Act of a Devoted Husband," December 29, 1883.

3. *The Whitesville News,* "THE MURDER OF LINCOLN," January 1, 1895.

4. Pitman, Benn. *The Assassination of President Lincoln and the Trial of the Conspirators David E. Herold, Mary E. Surratt, Lewis Payne, George A. Atzerodt, Edward Spangler, Samuel A. Mudd, Samuel Arnold, Michael O'Laughlin..* Cincinnati: Moore, Wilstach & Boldwin, 1865.

5. Edwards, William. *The Lincoln Assassination Trial - The Court Transcripts.* William Edwards, 2012.

6. *Troy Daily Times,* "Col. Rathbone' s Terrible Deed—Particulars of the Tragedy – An Insane Act of a Devoted Husband," December 29, 1883.

7. Surratt, John H., and George P. Fisher. *Trial of John H. Surratt in the Criminal Court for the District of Columbia, Hon. George P. Fisher presiding.* Washington [D.C.: Government Printing Office, 1867.

8. Henry, Guy Verner. *Military Record of Civilian Appointments in the United States Army.* New York: Carleton etc., 1869.

CHAPTER SEVEN

1. *Buffalo Evening News*, Vol. VII- No. 68, 12/31/1883.

2. *The Troy Daily Times* – Friday, July, 12 1867.

3. "A Tragedy That Blighted 2 More Lives." *Times Union* [Albany] 16 Apr. 1961: -. Print.

4. *Washington City, District of Columbia, City Directory*, 1870.

5. *The Evening Telegraph* (Philadelphia), "The Inaugural Procession-How it Will be Formed," March 3, 1869.

6. A Tragedy That Blighted 2 More Lives."Times Union [Albany] 16 Apr. 1961: -. Print.

7. *Troy Daily Times*, "Col. Rathbone's Terrible Deed—Particulars of the Tragedy – An Insane Act of a Devoted Husband," December 29, 1883.

8. "A Tragedy That Blighted 2 More Lives." *Times Union* [Albany] 16 Apr. 1961: -. Print.

9. *Evening Star.*, April 08, 1874.

10. Personal Letter from Committee on Alumni Records, Union College, J.R. Brown.

11. *Hopkinsville Kentuckian*, "Tragic Career of Maj. Rathbone Who Saw President Lincoln Killed," February 7, 1911.

12. "A Tragedy That Blighted 2 More Lives." *Times-Union* [Albany] 16 Apr. 1961: -. Print.

13. Savas, L. S., J. A. Cully, D. P. Graham, G. Tan, S. Laday Smith, S. Fitzgerald, K. Daci, M. Wieman, D. L. White, and H. B. El-Serag. "Irritable Bowel Syndrome And Dyspepsia Among Women Veterans: Prevalence And Association With Psychological Distress." *Alimentary Pharmacology & Therapeutics* 29.1 (2009): 115-125.

14. *Times-Union*, February, 11, 1959, p. 23.

15. *Evening Star.* November 29, 1878.

16. *The Daily Dispatch* (Richmond), "Mrs. Rathbone's Fate,"

January 2, 1884.

17. *Troy Daily Times,* "Col. Rathbone' s Terrible Deed — Particulars of the Tragedy – An Insane Act of a Devoted Husband," December 29, 1883.

18. *The Washington Post,* "The Rathbone Tragedy," December 30, 1883.

19. *Troy Daily Times,* "Col. Rathbone' s Terrible Deed — Particulars of the Tragedy – An Insane Act of a Devoted Husband," December 29, 1883.

20. IBID

21. IBID

22. *Hopkinsville Kentuckian,* "Tragic Career of Maj. Rathbone Who Saw President Lincoln Killed," February 7, 1911.

CHAPTER EIGHT

1. Friedman, Matthew. ""Soldier's Heart" and "Shell Shock:" Past Names for PTSD."Frontline. PBS, n.d. Web. 11 Oct. 2012. <http://www.pbs.org/wgbh/pages/frontline/shows/heart/themes/shellshock.html>.

2. Wiley, Bell Irvin. *The Life of Billy Yank: The Common Soldier of the Union.* Indianapolis: Bobbs-Merrill, 1952. Print.

3. Jones, Edgar, and Simon Wessely. "A paradigm shift in the conceptualization of psychological trauma in the 20th century." *Journal of Anxiety Disorders* 21, no. 2 (2007): 164-175.

4. *Diagnostic and Statistical Manual of Mental Disorders: DSM-5..* 5th ed. Washington, D.C.: American Psychiatric Association, 2013. Print.

5. *The Watchman and Southron,* March 03, 1887, Vol. VI. No. 31.

6. *Daily Saratogian,* Friday, 12/28/1883, Colonel Rathbone of Albany Shoots His Wife and Himself in Germany.

7. From *Troy Daily Times* – 12/29/1883, Col. Rathbone' s Terrible Deed—Particulars of the Tragedy – An Insane Act of a Devoted Husband

8. Friedman, Matthew J. "PTSD: National Center for PTSD." PTSD History and Overview. N.p., n.d. Web. 28 Sept. 2012. <http://www.ptsd.va.gov/professional/pages/ptsd-overview.asp>.

9. "Show Event | NGDC Natural Hazard Images | ngdc. noaa.gov." DECEMBER 7, 1988 LENINAKAN-SPITAK-KIROVAKAN ARMENIA EARTHQUAKE. NOAA, 12 Apr. 2013. Web. 31 Dec. 2013. <http://www.ngdc.noaa.gov/hazardimages/event/show/10>.

10. "Genes Linked to Post-Traumatic Stress Disorder." ScienceDaily. ScienceDaily, 2 Apr. 2012. Web. 10 Oct. 2012. <http://www.sciencedaily.com/releases/2012/04/120402093509.htm>.

11. "Gift From Within - PTSD Resources for Survivors and Caregivers." Guilt Following Traumatic Events. N.p., n.d. Web. 31 Dec. 2013. <http://www.giftfromwithin.org/html/Guilt-Following-Traumatic-Events.html>.

CHAPTER NINE

1. *The Daily Dispatch* (Richmond), "Mrs. Rathbone's Fate," January 2, 1884.

2. *New York Tribune* (New York), "Colonel Rathbone's Mania: What Hamilton Harris Says," December 31, 1883.

3. *The Daily Dispatch* (Richmond), "Mrs. Rathbone's Fate," January 2, 1884.

4. IBID

5. IBID

6. IBID

7. *New York Tribune* (New York), "Colonel Rathbone's Fatal Shot," December 29, 1883.

8. IBID

9. IBID

10. *The Daily Dispatch* (Richmond), "Mrs. Rathbone's Fate," January 2, 1884.

11. *New York Tribune* (New York), "Colonel Rathbone's Mania: What Hamilton Harris Says," December 31, 1883.

12. *New York Tribune* (New York), "Colonel Rathbone's Fatal Shot," December 29, 1883.

13. *Troy Daily Times*, "Col. Rathbone's Terrible Deed — Particulars of the Tragedy – An Insane Act of a Devoted Husband ," December 29, 1883.

14. *The Washington Post*, "The Rathbone Tragedy," December 30, 1883.

15. *New York Tribune* (New York), "Colonel Rathbone's Fatal Shot," December 29, 1883.

16. *New York Tribune* (New York), "Colonel Rathbone's Mania: What Hamilton Harris Says," December 31, 1883.

17. Roseberry, Cecil. "A Tragedy That Blighted 2 More Lives." *Times-Union* (Albany), April 16, 1961.

CHAPTER TEN

1. "A Teacher's Notes: Hildesheim and Harzburg." *Friends Intelligencer.* Philadelphia: Friends' Intelligencer Corporation, 1895. 526. Print.

2. Schauffler, Robert Haven. *Romantic Germany,*. New York: The Century co., 1909. Print.

3. Pension Evaluation Letter from Dr. A. Rosenbach, Oct. 13, 1891; Federal Military Pension Application- Civil War and Later Complete; National Archives Building, Washington, D.C.

4. *Daily Alta California,* Volume 42, Number 13983, 13 December 1887, Page 8.

5. *Syracuse Daily Journal,* 8/14/1911, Death Closes Tragic Career in Monastery.

6. *The Washington Times,* "Trustee for Lunatic Asked," October 2, 1903.

7. *The Washington Law Reporter.* Volume 34 ed. Washington, D.C.: Powell & Ginck, 1906.

8. *Albany Evening Journal,* "Major Rathbone's Death Expected," 1910.

9. "Medical Miscellany." *In Medical Art and Indianapolis Medical Journal,* volume 14, issue 11... Volume 14, Issue 3 ed. S.l.: Not Avail, 1911. 156.

10. *The Washington Times,* "Lincoln's Aide Leaves Estate Worth $70,870," September 9, 1912.

CPSIA information can be obtained at www.ICGtesting.com
Printed in the USA
BVOW04*0621010414

349330BV00001B/2/P